Saving Higher Education

The Integrated, Competency-Based Three-Year Bachelor's Degree Program

Martin J. Bradley
Robert H. Seidman
Steven R. Painchaud

JOSSEY-BASS
A Wiley Imprint
www.josseybass.com

The Jossey-Bass
Higher and Adult Education Series

Jossey-Bass books and products are available through most bookstores. To contact Jossey-Bass directly call our Customer Care Department within the U.S. at 800-956-7739, outside the U.S. at 317-572-3986, or fax 317-572-4002.

Wiley also publishes its books in a variety of electronic formats and by print-on-demand. Not all content that is available in standard print versions of this book may appear or be packaged in all book formats. If you have purchased a version of this book that did not include media that is referenced by or accompanies a standard print version, you may request this media by visiting http://booksupport.wiley.com. For more information about Wiley products, visit us www.wiley.com.

Library of Congress Cataloging-in-Publication Data

Bradley, Martin J.
    Saving higher education: the integrated, competency-based three-year bachelor's degree program / Martin J. Bradley, Robert H. Seidman, Steven R. Painchaud.
        p. cm.
    Includes bibliographical references and index.
    ISBN 978-0-470-88819-3 (cloth); ISBN 978-1-118-10646-4 (ebk.);
    ISBN 978-1-118-10647-1 (ebk.); ISBN 978-1-118-10648-8 (ebk.)
    1. Education, Higher–United States.   2. Educational change–United States.
I. Seidman, Robert H.   II. Painchaud, Steven R.   III. Title.
    LA227.4.B72 2012
    378.73–dc23   2011025955

Printed in the United States of America

FIRST EDITION

HB Printing   10 9 8 7 6 5 4 3 2 1

Contents

Additional Resources (available at http://www .josseybass.com/go/martinbradley):

Appendix 1: Sample Data Collection Course Form -
Course Topics/Learning Outcomes by
Program-Level Competencies
Appendix 2: Sample Tabulation of Topics/Learning
Outcomes by Course and Program Competencies

We dedicate this book to our spouses—Michelle D. Bradley, Robin Seidman, and Maria Manus Painchaud—and our children Matthew, Michael, and Justin Bradley and Elena and Mark Painchaud. Their love and support means everything to us.

List of Tables and Figures

Preface

American higher education is at the breaking point. It is at a critical crossroads, with the very survival of many institutions at stake. The current price structure has become unsustainable for many students and their families, and costs have become problematic for a great many higher educational institutions as well. Additionally, employers often express concerns that many college graduates are not sufficiently prepared to enter the workforce and succeed in today's knowledge economy. There is fierce competition between traditional nonprofit and for-profit educational institutions to attract students seeking to earn a college degree without having to sink deeply into debt. Data reported by Knapp, Kelly-Reid, and Ginder in *Postsecondary Institutions and Price of Attendance in the United States* (2010) show that in 2008–2009, for-profit institutions enrolled almost 11 percent of the higher education U.S. student population, a 20 percent increase from the previous academic year. Between 2004–2005 and 2008–2009, the increase was 60 percent.

It is becoming increasingly clear that without fundamental changes, a college education will soon be out of reach for many more of our citizens. This could harm our nation's ability to compete effectively in a global marketplace, slow the advancement of knowledge, and diminish the quality of life for many individuals and families as well as society as a whole.

It has long been recognized that higher education is an important vehicle for achieving economic success and improved social prosperity in the United States. Carnevale's (2008) analyses show that bachelor's degree attainment grew significantly when colleges and universities enjoyed long periods of growth in the second half of the twentieth century. Other studies argue convincingly that higher education remains one of the few industries in which consumer demand and competition has had only a marginal effect on price and cost controls (Zemsky, Wegner, & Massy, 2005; Archibald & Feldman, 2010). Today's students and their families are being asked to make enormous financial sacrifices in the pursuit of higher education in order to prepare for life and work in the twenty-first century. Something is very wrong when a college education costs as much as many typical middle-class families earn annually. It is clear that controlling tuition and institutional costs while at the same time delivering high-quality educational experiences that meet individual and societal needs is key to the continued success of postsecondary education in the United States. The stakes are incredibly high.

With this book, we want to change the nature of the conversation about three-year bachelor's degrees, which in turn may alter the future cost-price trajectory of higher education. Several three-year-degree models exist, but only one, the Integrated Three-Year Model, can save students and their families 25 percent of the price they pay for higher education while at the same time saving institutions almost that much in delivery costs. Most importantly, the savings realized by this model can be accomplished without diminishing the quality of the educational experience for the students.

We adopt the distinction between the cost and price of education that Archibald and Feldman make in their book *Why Does College Cost So Much?* (2010). *Price* refers to what the students pay for tuition, fees, and room and board. *Cost* refers to the value of resources used by the institution to provide the education.

This book describes a highly integrated, competency-based three-year model that challenges the long-standing notion that seat time is inextricably linked to educational attainment. Instead, the new model relies on demonstrated competency attainment supported by a highly integrated curriculum structure to ensure a quality education. Although some of the model's components are not new, what is novel is the way in which they are embedded in a curriculum structure that reduces the traditional eight college semesters to six while maintaining 120 earned credits.

The Integrated Model fundamentally changes the way that higher education institutions can successfully deliver undergraduate education. We can say this unequivocally because we have been affiliated with just such a program since 1997, when Southern New Hampshire University admitted its first three-year-degree class. Since then, students in this integrated program have been earning a full 120 credits in six semesters—without weekend, night, summer, or intersession classes. Research results show that these students achieve at levels at least as high as their nationally normed four-year counterparts on an ETS Major Field Test.

Saving Higher Education: The Integrated, Competency-Based Three-Year Bachelor's Degree Program is not meant to be a case study, although the ideas put forward have been tested over many years. Instead, this book describes a general three-year integrated model in such a way that interested readers can decide for themselves what it would take to transform their own existing four-year undergraduate programs. The new model applies to a wide variety of institutions and programs and will appeal to those who have an abiding interest in the future of higher education in general and of their own institutions in particular. This group includes college and university presidents, chief financial officers, and enrollment executives who are concerned about the escalating price of a college degree and their institution's ability to meet its enrollment and retention targets given their revenue and cost structure. The group also includes provosts, chief academic officers, deans, department chairs, and faculty from a variety of disciplines who want to develop innovative, high-quality academic programs that better prepare students for life and work in the twenty-first century, meet the calls from internal and external stakeholders to demonstrate student outcomes, and reduce time to graduation. Government officials and politicians at all levels will be interested in this model because of its cost savings and its emphasis on student learning outcomes.

The title of this book might at first blush appear to be a bit presumptuous, to say the least. You will see in the chapters that follow that no one claims that the Integrated Three-Year Model alone is a silver bullet that can save the massive enterprise that is U.S. higher education. Institutions will continue to teeter on the edge of financial insolvency and some, perhaps many, will fall. What the book seeks to demonstrate is a way to realize savings in the price students pay and the cost to institutions; together these savings could bring the higher education price-cost trajectory under control. It is at this price-cost nexus that institutions large and small, lacking sufficient endowments, can avoid pricing themselves out of reach and can potentially attract and keep students who will be able to afford the quality of higher education that they want, need, and deserve.

A three-year bachelor's degree may not be for everyone. Certainly, some students enter college with little or no idea of what they want to study and wait until the end of their first or second year to declare a major. A four-year program is better suited for them. But there is no reason why three-year programs can't coexist with four-year programs and help to deliver institutional cost savings and student price reductions. This book includes an example of one such program, and as the reader will see, it has, among other things, significantly increased student retention for more than a decade.

Outline of Contents

Three-year degrees are not new in American higher education, and *Chapter 1* places the three-year-degree movement into a historical perspective. The chapter discusses the three Cs that are the central forces contributing to renewed interest in three-year degrees: cost, competition, and curriculum innovation. Three contemporary three-year-degree models are described: Accelerated, Prior Learning, and Integrated Competency-Based. The reader is challenged to think differently about higher education, and three-year degrees are placed in a global context, which includes discussion of the Bologna agreement. The chapter also includes a comparison table of the seven main attributes of the three three-year models. Chapter 7 discusses the comparisons in detail.

Chapter 2 discusses two of the three underlying core elements of the Integrated Three-Year Model: (1) the elimination of seat time as a primary measure of student learning and delivery of education and (2) a competency-based curriculum that focuses on measurable learning outcomes at the school, program, and course levels.

Chapter 3 focuses on the third core element: (3) educational experiences that align with program-level competencies. A multipart method for accomplishing the redesign demonstrates how integrated academic experiences tie competencies together and how academic plans ensure competency alignment at the school, program, and course levels.

The very best academic program is worthless unless it can be implemented successfully. *Chapter 4* explains the Integrated Three-Year Model's implementation framework and its challenges. Integrated three-year programs have implementation challenges that other programs do not have. This chapter describes a change model as well as the resistance one can expect from a project like this. However, the rewards for perseverance can be substantial.

Does the Integrated Three-Year-Degree Model actually work? *Chapter 5* is a proof-of-concept chapter that focuses on Southern New Hampshire University's (SNHU) experience with this model. The results and analyses of financial considerations for students and their families and for higher education institutions are covered. Also covered are the results and analyses of student academic performance, retention, graduation rates, workforce readiness, and student life. The guiding notion here is that the transition from a four-year program to a three-year program need not, indeed must not, reduce the quality of education.

What kind of value-added dimensions contribute to the success of the Integrated Three-Year-Degree Model? *Chapter 6* describes a number of leading dimensions: student cohorts and learning communities, study groups and work groups, academic themes, and professional learning communities of practice. Other value-added dimensions are active teaching and learning paradigms, virtual collaborative learning environments, and assessment of student competency achievement. The chapter walks the reader through the first year from student and faculty points of view. An outline of the second year and a detailed walk-through of the third and final year of a student's program conclude the chapter.

Chapter 1 introduced three types of three-year models. *Chapter 7* compares core elements, value-added dimensions, and implementation challenges of the Integrated Model and the Accelerated and Prior Learning Models.

Key questions about the integrated model are presented in *Chapter 8* via a question-and-answer format. This chapter addresses major concerns that readers might have about the Integrated Three-Year Model and engages them in a dialogue to expose some of the less obvious ramifications of the model and to reinforce some of the most important ones.

Three-year-degree programs are one thing, but a three-year university is quite another thing altogether. *Chapter 9* discusses the key design principles and challenges of a three-year university. It is an outline of what it would take for schools within a university, or an entire university itself, to adopt an Integrated Three-Year Model for most, if not all, of its programs. The chapter also discusses how a three-year university built upon the Integrated Three-Year Model could increase the knowledge and skills college students gain.

The *appendices* contain many documents and forms to help illuminate and facilitate the process of transforming standard four-year programs into integrated three-year academic programs.

A. Colleges and Universities Offering Three-Year-Degree Programs

B. National Graduation and Retention Statistics

C. Academic Plan for Three-Year Communications Module

D. Academic Plan for Three-Year Management Module

E. Model Syllabus for Three-Year Human Relations Module

F. Flowchart of the Three-Year Bachelor of Science in Business Administration Development Activities

G. The SNHU Three-Year Program Mission Statement

Martin J. Bradley
Robert H. Seidman
Steven R. Painchaud
Manchester, New Hampshire

Acknowledgments

We are very grateful to the many dedicated former and current faculty and professional and support staff members at Southern New Hampshire University whose contributions to developing and nurturing an integrated, competency-based three-year degree program over the past sixteen years made this book possible. We salute the many three-year-degree students who have graduated from the program and those we have had the pleasure of teaching.

In particular, we offer special recognition to the contributions made by Dr. Robert Losik in the early design phase of this program—his creativity and energy was unmatched. Dr. C. Richard Erskine enthusiastically read multiple drafts of our work—his insightful comments and suggestions made our manuscript better. Our heartfelt appreciation goes to Mrs. Karla Lamphere, who joined the three-year design team support staff in 1996 and worked tirelessly over this past year on the manuscript's structure and layout.

We thank the members of the original design team and steering committee: Dr. Robert Begiebing, Dr. Robert Craven, Dr. Robert Doucette, Professor Eleanor Dunfey-Freiburger, Dr. Robert Losik, the late Professor Richard Pantano, Ms. Jacqueline Ribaudo, and Professor Carol West. Our thanks also go out to Dr. Richard Gustafson, Dr. Jacqueline F. Mara, Dr. Steven Harvey, Ms. Polly St. Hilaire, Ms. Karen D'Bate, Mr. Brad Poznanski, and Mr. Edward M. Shapiro. For their long-time support, thanks to Dr. Jack Evans,

Mrs. Ashley Liadis, Ms. Patricia Gerard, Dr. Ronald Biron, and Mrs. Patricia Shrader as well as to Dr. Tej Dhakar and Dr. Kishore Pochampally for their assistance with the statistical analyses in the book. Thanks also to our friends at Fidelity Investments, Mr. Jim Hecker of Fitz Vogt Associates, Mr. Jean Michaud of Kaleidoscope Inc., Mr. Rene Drouin of the New Hampshire Higher Education Assistance Foundation, and others too numerous to name.

We are appreciative of the excellent research support we received from Danielle Cross, Janessa Gray, and Elena Painchaud. And we are deeply appreciative for the support we received from the Southern New Hampshire University administration for this book project.

Finally, we are also thankful for the expert guidance given to us by the editorial staff at Jossey-Bass, especially Aneesa Davenport, who was the steward on the publishing process.

About the Authors

Martin J. Bradley was the principal investigator of the U.S. Department of Education Fund for the Improvement of Postsecondary Education (FIPSE) three-year-degree grant awarded in 1995 to Southern New Hampshire University (then called New Hampshire College). He was the first director of the Three-Year Program and then the dean of the SNHU School of Business, where the program resides administratively. He has taught in the program since its inception. Bradley won the university's highest teaching award in 2001 and was recognized as Outstanding Professor for the State of New Hampshire in 2002. Bradley is now professor of Organizational Leadership at SNHU.

Robert H. Seidman was a member of the FIPSE grant team that created the Integrated Three-Year-Degree Program at SNHU in 1996. He has taught in the program and has been a steering committee member continuously since its inception. He is a professor of Computer Information Technology, executive editor of the *Journal of Educational Computing Research*, joint author of *Predicting the Behavior of the Educational System* (1990), coauthor of *Fluency with Alice* (2009), and author of numerous journal articles and book chapters. He was the Southern New Hampshire University Faculty Scholar for the 2010–2011 academic year. His website is http://bit.ly/DrRHSeidman.

Steven R. Painchaud has taught in the Three-Year Program since its inception and has played a key role in the year one end-of-semester integrating experience. Now a professor of Organizational Leadership, he served for fifteen years as the associate dean of the Graduate School of Business before joining the faculty in 2000. Painchaud received the highest honor of the Accreditation Council for Business Schools and Programs (ACBSP) for excellence in teaching and is a longstanding member of the three-year-degree steering committee. His daughter completed the three-year-degree program in 2008.

The Need for Change

Why Some Institutions Will Embrace New Pathways to the Bachelor's Degree

While the system of American higher education has evolved, important aspects of curriculum design and instruction have gone largely untouched for over two centuries. The social contract was, and still is, for families to send their sons and daughters to the university for a set number of years of study during which time the family would find ways to pay for the cost of the education. At the end of the college experience, the university would declare the student educated and prepared to contribute to society in a variety of meaningful ways.

The college investment, particularly through the twentieth century, yielded great opportunities for the college graduate. As the country developed, more educated and sound thinkers were required to ensure that the economy prospered. This same intellectual capital was a requisite for economic expansion of the twentieth century and fueled tremendous growth in postsecondary education.

As more and more people sought access to postsecondary education, leaders looked for ways to run their universities as cost-effective organizations. At the start of the twenty-first century, these challenges still exist as tuition and ancillary costs continue to spiral up, threatening middle-class access to higher education. This is the same middle class that fueled the unprecedented expansion in the twentieth century. These barriers are now threatening the very existence of some colleges and universities.

Students and their families are being asked to make enormous financial investments as they prepare for life and work in the twenty-first century. Unlike many professions and industries, where growth in customers and overall expansion often translates into lower costs, this has not been true for the labor-intensive business models of American higher education. The delivery model has changed little over the last two hundred years. It remains highly labor-intensive in an enterprise that is widely recognized as slow to embrace change (Noble, 2002). It is a model where most commonly the professor is the purveyor of knowledge and the students are the passive recipients of the educational experience. So challenging are the problems of cost containment and quality that Gordon Gee, president of Ohio State University, has called for "radical reformation" in the way colleges and universities are organized and operate (Fain, 2009). The choice, he says, is either "reinvention or extinction." Gee echoes what has become a growing chorus of leaders expressing deep concern over the mounting difficulties of access to and the quality of the higher educational system.

American higher education is at a crucial juncture, with the viability of many institutions at stake. Further, the current expense structure is forcing many students and their families to consider alternative approaches for pursuing higher education (Zemsky, Wegner, & Massy, 2005). Employers are increasingly concerned that college graduates are not sufficiently prepared to enter the workforce and succeed in the knowledge economy (Alexander, 2009). And there is increasingly fierce competition between traditional nonprofit colleges and universities and for-profit educational institutions to attract students seeking to earn a college degree without going too deeply into debt. The *Condition of Education 2011* reports that 27 percent of the increase in undergraduate enrollments from 2000 to 2009 was at private for-profit institutions (Aud et al., 2011, p. 7).

The Integrated Three-Year-Degree Model presented in this book is a proven path that institutions can take to control and reduce costs, to offer a curriculum more responsive to the needs of society and business, and to more effectively compete for students. Integrated degree programs can achieve these ends without sacrificing educational quality while at the same time enhancing institutional retention efforts.

It is becoming increasingly clear that unless fundamental changes occur soon, there is a growing danger of putting a college education out of reach for more and more of our citizens. This could have profound effects upon the nation's ability to compete in a global marketplace and negatively affect the advancement of knowledge.

The Three Cs: Cost, Competition, and Curriculum Innovation

Cost Structures Are Unsustainable

When a college education can cost as much or more than a typical middle-class family earns in one year, there is cause for concern. We know that higher education has been a primary vehicle for improved economic and social prosperity. Yet, if the cost of pursuing a college degree continues to spiral up unabated, what has become a rite of passage for many middle-class students will cease to be a realistic option. And if this occurs, many tuition-driven colleges and universities will close their doors due to the deadly combination of declining enrollments and rising costs.

With increasing frequency, traditional and nontraditional students at the graduate and undergraduate level are opting to complete degrees in both hybrid and fully asynchronous course formats (Perry, 2010). This change in preference bodes well for those for-profit institutions that emphasize speed and convenience as a prime draw for students. However, it also puts additional pressure on nonprofit colleges and universities offering the traditional four-year undergraduate experience. Although many of these institutions now offer online educational opportunities, the financial investment required to build the necessary online capacity often means diverting limited resources from other important areas. These shifts in student preferences and the significant investment needed to achieve and maintain capacity will result in the demise of a number of institutions, particularly those with little or no margin for error.

The ability of colleges and universities to control the escalating price of tuition is obviously crucial for their survival. Yet cost containment alone is not sufficient to ensure their long-term viability. They must also be able to deliver a high-quality education where their graduates attain the knowledge and skills (that is, competencies), necessary to succeed in today's knowledge economy. And the awarding of a degree will no longer alone suffice as evidence that the necessary knowledge and skills were attained. Colleges and universities will need to develop assessment measures that clearly demonstrate the competency achievements of their graduates.

As more three-year-degree programs become available, many students will recognize the financial advantage of entering the workforce one year earlier than their four-year counterparts. The opportunity to gain a competitive advantage in the workplace will make the integrated three-year degree an even more attractive option.

Increasing Competition

Students and their families have choices, and academic major and geographic proximity are no longer the most compelling factors in selecting a college. Further, as the many nonprofits that lack brand awareness in their local markets lose enrollments to for-profit institutions, financial pressures will be further exacerbated. Higher education leaders will be forced to think in new ways in order to ensure institutional survival. For many, this means continuing to increase the annual financial aid awards, resulting in a 40–50 percent or higher discount on the annual tuition cost. Only a decade ago, such a discount rate would have been denounced as financially irresponsible. Although this discount practice may support a short-term enrollment jump, the long-term effects will surely only make these institutions more financially vulnerable, particularly when compared to well-financed for-profit educational institutions.

Increasingly, institutions are now offering accelerated three-year-degree programs that allow students to complete a 120-credit-hour bachelor's degree (for example, forty three-credit courses) within thirty-six months. Further, many institutions that allow students to complete their degree in three years are not charging additional tuition for earlier completion, essentially giving these students a year's worth of coursework for free. Therefore, for institutions that have aggressively discounted financial aid to all students and now offer a free year's worth of tuition to students participating in an accelerated three-year-degree program, the effective discount rate will be in excess of 65 percent. This is absolutely unsustainable! Desperation is clearly driving the decision making of these institutions. Rather than focusing on discounting tuition, institutional leaders would do well to embrace new models that would afford their institution the opportunity to operate in innovative ways and create new value for the many stakeholders that make up the institution's accountability network.

The real opportunity comes when institutions offer programs and services that the general public views as necessary. The Integrated Three-Year-Degree Model is one proven example of how to create a new space from which to compete and operate, thus attracting students who seek new educational experiences. What we know is that students need learning experiences that yield identifiable and measurable outcomes, or as has been discussed, a set of appropriate competencies. No matter the profession or industry, building value for stakeholders while competing successfully takes a disciplined leadership unit that embraces change and recognizes that the competitive forces in American higher education have forever changed.

Curriculum Reform through an Integrated, Competency-Based Program Can Assure High Quality

To successfully rethink traditional measures such as seat time or contact hours, an appropriate substitute must be used, such as competencies. It is remarkable what can happen when the bond is broken between credit and seat time. Now, credits can be based upon learning outcomes rather than hours spent in the classroom. An integrated, competency-based program that is predicated upon achieving certain knowledge and skills allows the redesign of a four-year curriculum so that it can be delivered in three years without any dilution of academic quality and at a cost savings for both students and the institution (more discussion of seat time appears in Chapters 2 and 6).

While this is easier said than done, nevertheless, data supports the notion that an integrated three-year program based on competency and learning outcomes can deliver a high-quality education to students in six semesters without additional semester, summer, or weekend courses. The challenge is to identify the set of competencies and to organize and deliver a curriculum that aligns learning activities with these competencies. Moreover, robust assessment procedures are needed to assure that all the learning goals are properly met.

Implementing an integrated, competency-based three-year-degree program can be best facilitated when educational leaders and faculty rethink the process of teaching and learning. Everyone must be willing to challenge traditional assumptions about the roles of faculty and students so that faculty acting in concert can create greater integration throughout their academic disciplines. This, together with students taking greater responsibility for managing their own education, can go a long way toward ensuring the success of the program.

This kind of rethinking includes a renewed emphasis on student acquisition of knowledge and skills (that is, competencies) and greater emphasis on measuring and demonstrating learning outcomes. To achieve this, there must be a commitment to engage in ongoing internal and external assessment efforts. Colleges and universities must develop and implement a comprehensive set of formative and summative evaluation measures to demonstrate that students are achieving the intended outcomes and that the curriculum content of the new model is both relevant and responsive to the needs of society. Data and analyses from these assessment efforts need to be widely shared with interested stakeholders, particularly students and their families.

A number of important value-added dimensions can help ensure the success of an integrated, competency-based three-year model. The synergy produced by incorporating student cohorts and learning communities along with faculty learning communities, academic themes, virtual collaborative environments, and active teaching and learning can go a long way toward successful program implementation.

In short, an integrated, competency-based three-year-degree model is a viable and attractive approach for addressing the three Cs: meeting cost challenges while maintaining academic quality and addressing concerns about the preparedness of graduates. The three-year model also addresses the challenges that families face in affording a bachelor's degree.

A Look Back

As Allen (1973) reminds us, the three-year-degree discussion today is not a new one. Indeed, midway through the nineteenth century, Harvard and Yale had each launched formal three-year-degree programs. One of their motives was to respond to growing concerns that American higher education was in need of structural changes. Some people argued that not everyone should be required to complete four years of college-level training. For the remainder of the nineteenth century and the first three decades of the twentieth century, new institutions such as Johns Hopkins, Clark University, University of Chicago, and Antioch College all pondered how to design the undergraduate experience. In fact, President William Rainey Harper of the University of Chicago suggested that any structural change should include the secondary education system as well as postsecondary education (Brubacher & Rudy, 1976).

Both Johns Hopkins and Clark University began by offering graduate-level programs. Johns Hopkins moved rapidly to develop undergraduate programs, while Clark University waited for well over a decade before more cautiously doing so. Its first program, interestingly enough, was a three-year-degree program. At the University of Chicago, President Harper was in favor of offering some form of a redesigned curriculum, but he was not in favor of a three-year-degree offering. Rather, the university needed to recognize that students would bring to the institution different needs and desires (Allen, 1973). Antioch College began with a very interesting yet different model: the academic year was broken into blocks of academic study followed by an equal period when students would work full-time. This approach demonstrated a clear commitment to the importance of both theory and practice (Brubacher & Rudy, 1976).

Much of the fourth, fifth, and sixth decades of the twentieth century were marked by war and social upheaval, but it was also a time when American higher education experienced tremendous growth across all facets of the academy. This period, 1945–1975, has been referred to as the golden age (Cohen & Kisker, 2010). With this growth came much discussion about curriculum and instructional innovation and the need for structural reform. One of many topics revisited at this time was idea of the three-year baccalaureate degree.

Allen (1973) reported in an article titled "The 3 Year Baccalaureate" that thirty colleges and universities were offering three-year programs in 1973, and another nineteen institutions were considering such programs. Clearly, at least the perceived need for a new pathway had gained the attention of many educational leaders by the mid-1970s. On further review of these programs, Allen found that they all fell within one of four categories: the compression model, the early admission model, the credit-by-examination model, and the restructuring model.

The compression model, as Allen (1973) states, "is not a new curricular contribution" (p. 67). Rather, it is a well-worn approach whereby students complete the curriculum at a faster pace. The early admission model is comparable to what is referred to today as the dual enrollment or concurrent enrollment program. This approach allows high school students to complete college-level courses for credit. These arrangements are specific between colleges and universities and individual private high schools or public school districts. Currently there are dozens of partnerships across the United States as well as a number of pieces of pending legislation calling for more opportunities to be made available to a larger pool of students. The credit-by-examination approach allows high school students to sit for select national exams. Many might recognize this approach in today's environment as the advanced placement process and referred to as "AP credit." The final approach, the restructuring model, clearly requires the most radical changes in the curriculum. This approach requires educational leaders to support a complete overhaul, or restructuring, of the curriculum. In today's curriculum language, this approach most closely aligns with the Integrated, Competency-Based Model that is discussed throughout this book.

New Model Needed

The challenge and opportunity for today's university leaders is to consider new ways to create a learning environment that embraces the best practices from other countries and industries and ensures that the intellectual potential of students can be maximized while controlling costs and protecting academic integrity (Twigg, 2003). New models and constructs are needed in order to conceive different pathways for learning and degree attainment. What also seems apparent is that the changes occurring across the academy will not be limited to the traditional 18- to 22-year-old undergraduate population. Indeed, the degree-attainment opportunities for adult learners will also undergo changes in the years ahead, with some of these changes facilitated by technological advancements and others by increased and intense competition among institutions for enrollments across delivery systems (Dolence & Norris, 1995).

The expansion of the Internet coupled with heavy investments by colleges and universities in technology infrastructure have positioned many campuses to become sophisticated content distributors, offering courses and degrees available anytime and anywhere around the world. This shift in delivery strategy is shattering the traditional face-to-face delivery model that has influenced and produced generations of graduates. This shift is forcing institutional leaders, especially those of small and endowment-poor colleges, to seek new models that will allow them to maintain financial viability while controlling costs so that access for students remains readily available. Although online education has dominated the landscape in recent years and shows no signs of slowing down, other programmatic ideas have been proposed for years and are now just being implemented. Indeed, Senator Lamar Alexander, a former university president and U.S. Secretary of Education, suggests that it is time for colleges and universities to find ways to cut costs by thinking in different ways such as offering three-year-degree programs (Alexander, 2009; Lederman, 2009).

Three-Year-Degree Models

Implementing three-year-degree curricula is not a new idea. As reported by Allen (1973), institutions have examined this issue at different periods over the last 150 years. In fact, several schools, such as Hartwick College and Bates College, have offered three-year programs for many years (Keller, 2008).

Today, three-year programs have been slow to catch on even though "this recession has lasted longer than the median length of the 10 previous recessions that have occurred since World War II" (Labonte, 2009). Prior to 2010, fewer than thirty colleges and universities offered three-year-degree programs, and all but one were degree options that offered either an accelerated program or a prior-experience format. Appendix A provides an up-to-date listing of three-year-degree programs at the time of publication. Table 1.1 presents an overview of the approaches that provide an opportunity for students to complete their bachelor's degree in three years. The table examines each of the models from the vantage point of seven key attributes, which will be discussed in detail in Chapter 7 along with the strengths and weaknesses of each of the three-year-degree models.

Accelerated Three-Year Model

The accelerated approach is attractive for institutions because it requires little change in the way that educational content is designed and delivered to students. Typically, the compression of content takes the form of delivering traditional courses in less time, thus requiring students to accelerate seat time during a shorter delivery window. Further acceleration often appears in the requirements to complete a particular program of study. Examples include taking classes through some nontraditional means, such as nights, weekends, summers, online, and intersession terms. One obvious benefit of an accelerated option to students is that they are able to complete a bachelor's degree in three years. Supporters of the accelerated approach point to the fact that graduates are able to enter the workforce a year before their contemporaries. Yet at many institutions that offer the accelerated model, students still must pay the four-year tuition price; a few examples are Lipscomb University, Florida State University, and the University of South Dakota. In a sense, students are permitted to use a faster conveyor belt in order to complete program requirements but at no real cost savings, except ancillary expenses such as room and board of the extra year in school.

Institutions that choose to charge only three years of tuition effectively bear the costs of providing four years' worth of resources

Table 1.1. Institutional Comparisons and Implications of Three-Year-Degree Models

Program Attributes	Accelerated Curriculum Model	Prior Learning Model	Integrated Curriculum Model
View of the Curriculum	Curriculum advancements are marginal and incremental.	Curriculum credit for prior learning is awarded through a variety of methods.	Curriculum advancements are a breakthrough.
Curriculum Restructuring or Redesign	No integration of curriculum—focus remains on seat time.	No integration of curriculum in spite of recognition of the importance of prior learning experiences.	Integrated curriculum—focus is on "learning" and the demonstration of competencies.
Administrative Needs for the Program	The focus is on management activities and fits with the current administrative/business model.	The focus is on administrative review and related activities required to certify prior learning.	The focus is on systems changes and leadership activities and requires a new view of the administrative/business model.
Enrollment Strategy Approach	The institution (in some cases) cuts profit margins in order to compete for new enrollments.	The institution generates little if any revenue from the review of prior learning content but attracts new enrollments.	The institution protects profit margins and competes in a new space that brings in new and different students.

Leadership View	Institutional leaders resist change and are wedded to traditional delivery models and cost structures.	Institutional leaders view the process of prior learning as an administrative activity.	Institutional leaders see opportunities that come with embracing change and implementing new delivery models that promote new revenue streams.
Cost Structure	The degree path (course work) is faster, yet delivery costs are similar or the same; in some cases, the institution waives the revenue of the final ten courses.	The degree path is faster in that students may receive credit for up to ten courses (some institutions may even permit more), thus saving tuition expense and time.	The degree path is different and faster, yet delivery costs are significantly reduced.
Savings for Students and Families	No change in the continued rising costs of postsecondary education; in most cases little or no savings is passed on to families.	If students qualify, they could save time and financial resources.	A key shift in the way postsecondary education is organized and delivered, with savings passed on to families.

but reap revenue for only three. This is a financial loss for the university although a savings for the students. This is also a potentially risky practice in that as three-year programs grow in popularity, students who remain on a four-year track will demand the same discount afforded to their three-year counterparts. Some of the many institutions engaging in this practice include Grace College in Indiana, Arcadia University in Pennsylvania, and Lynn University in Florida.

Prior-Experience Three-Year Model

A model that differs from the accelerated option gives students credit for prior knowledge and life experience. The amount of credit is determined by some form of prior-learning assessment (PLA). The Council for Adult and Experiential Learning (CAEL, 2009) defines PLA as "the process by which many colleges evaluate for academic credit the college-level knowledge and skills an individual has gained outside of the classroom." This is similar to using a College-Level Examination Program (CLEP) to assess acquired knowledge. Other types of assessment include portfolios, evaluation of training programs via the American Council on Education (ACE), advanced placement (AP) exams, and institutional exams developed by subject-matter experts on the faculty. A major advantage of the PLA approach is that students receive credit toward degree completion without the tuition expense or seat time, although they may still incur small fees to cover the cost of administration and processing. This model has limited viability because only a select group of students is able to qualify.

Integrated, Competency-Based Three-Year Model

The third model employs an integrated, competency-based curriculum approach. A predetermined set of competencies are foundational to the students' educational experience. In addition to the set of competencies, the curriculum is redesigned and integrated wherever possible to maximize student learning opportunities throughout their entire educational experience. Teaching faculty that participate in the program receive an orientation outlining the curriculum design and are mindful of the program competencies, as well as accreditation standards and expectations. Utilizing a collaborative approach, faculty members deliver courses over a period of six semesters (120 credits), with no summer sessions or winter intersessions needed. The content is configured in a way that facilitates collaboration by faculty across disciplines.

The competencies serve as guideposts for the content of all the academic experiences within the curriculum. Because the development of competencies occurs at varying levels of intensity throughout the three years, a key strategy is the use of master planning documents for each academic experience. For each of the educational experiences, an academic plan is developed that details the overarching strategy for addressing the competencies within the experience along with specific implementing activities that the faculty can employ. These academic plans are regularly reviewed and updated as part of an ongoing assessment of the program. The academic plans serve as the basis for the development of model syllabi that demonstrate the relationship between the academic requirements, assignments, and the competencies.

For reasons that will become evident in Chapters 2 and 3, we use the term *module* instead of *course* when speaking of the integrated three-year-degree program. Each module that a student takes has an academic plan developed by faculty experts. These academic plans provide a strategic framework allowing faculty, administrators, accreditation organizations, and other interested parties to see how each of the courses in a given semester or year support the program-level competencies and learning outcomes. These academic plans and model syllabi are discussed further in Chapter 3.

Each semester concludes with an innovative week-long, credit-bearing "integrating experience." These experiences place students in academic work teams in which they are given challenging case-based problems related to their major. Teaching faculty hold special consulting hours to provide guidance and support to the student teams.

Integration of academic content throughout the three years is achieved in a number of ways, including program themes, joint assignments across modules and between various disciplines, end-of-semester integrating experiences, and experiential learning opportunities. During the last week of each of the first four semesters, students engage in a team-intensive activity exercising their newly acquired knowledge and skills to address real-world case studies. Each experience focuses on the competencies stressed during the semester and culminates with a formal presentation to the faculty and invited members from the internal university community as well as invited guests.

Accelerated versus Integrated, Competency-Based Models

A major perceived advantage of the accelerated three-year model is that very little curriculum modification needs to occur. In fact, in most instances the curriculum does not change at all. Only the time frame for delivering the curriculum is modified in order to meet the thirty-six-month timetable. So for traditional institutions, launching an accelerated curriculum might be politically feasible although it might not be the most attractive scenario for potential students. Because curriculum changes can be very time-consuming and must navigate various university governance mechanisms, working with a curriculum that is already in place more easily meets faculty needs and stays within many administrators' comfort zone.

On the other hand, designing and implementing an integrated, competency-based, or outcomes-focused, curriculum model requires faculty to collaborate and to be flexible in their pedagogical approaches. An integrated model requires that traditional courses be thought of in new ways, such as modules that are premised upon the principles of student knowledge acquisition and skill development. Further, an integrated curriculum is premised on a set of programmatic and school-based competencies. These competencies influence and in some cases drive the choices of content acquisition, delivery, and demonstration.

Building an integrated curriculum can by its very nature be labor-intensive and will likely meet with resistance at some institutions. On the other hand, creating an integrated curriculum can inspire faculty to collaborate and think of education in new ways, such as placing the student at the center of learning (Barr & Tagg, 1995; Tagg, 2003). Implementing an integrated curriculum also demands that administrators think in new ways regarding programmatic delivery needs such as classroom space, awarding of credit hours, and the coordination of the course registration processes. The curriculum redesign also requires the support of key institutional leaders in order for the curriculum to survive the academic governance process.

Changing the Way We Think about Higher Education

Changing the way we think about the design and delivery of the higher education experience demands that university leaders think in new ways. This means that modules will look different in an integrated curriculum than in a traditional three-credit, one-hour-and-15-minutes, twice-per-week course. For example, faculty may deem it educationally beneficial for students to spend more class time on a particular subject area. Thus the module might be delivered in a two-hour class that meets four days a week over seven weeks as opposed to the more typical two-day-a-week, one-hour-and-15-minute class that meets for fifteen weeks.

Accelerated-curriculum models fit more easily into a traditional administrative mindset because typical tuition and seat-time practices remain undisturbed. On the other hand, an integrated curriculum requires administrative leaders who are willing to break decades of traditional practices in order to create new value for their students. Providing the leadership to promote true innovation is no easy task. As Collins (2001) reminds us, "good is the enemy of great," and many institutional administrators are happy to be just "good enough."

One of the clear challenges facing university presidents and other senior leaders is to envision new ways in which to construct the college experience—ways that promote learning and create new value for their students. Successfully meeting this challenge requires a willingness to examine long-held assumptions regarding administrative practices such as credit hours and seat time. Instead, a new focus on learning, competency attainment, and demonstration should drive how we design and deliver the curriculum.

As competition increases, more colleges and universities will look to offer new ways for students to earn a bachelor's degree. The accelerated model will be attractive given that initially, institutions will see the model as a means of retaining tuition income because students will be required to complete the same number of courses. Yet many universities already offer full-time students the option of adding up to one course above the standard load (that is, six instead of five three-credit courses per semester) at no additional cost. These students can shave six courses off the total in six semesters, thereby needing to complete the remaining four courses by some alternative means, such as night school, intersession term, and summers.

In these scenarios, institutions will lose tuition revenue without cutting delivery costs, thus speeding up the downward financial spiral. Many institutions will need more students in order to balance their budget. Thus, many small, less-selective institutions will experience increased pressure to lower entrance requirements as a means of attracting more students. At the same time, these institutions will feel growing pressure from the competition whose size or scale will continue to increase price pressure in the market place—pricing more cheaply for credit courses.

Reducing Price for Students and Costs to Institutions

The integrated, competency-based model will be particularly attractive and useful to small and mid-sized institutions that seek to enhance current enrollments or that are interested in attracting new enrollment segments. In the subsequent chapters, readers will learn how institutions can launch an integrated, competency-based program that reduces delivery costs.

This book puts forth an already proven model of a three-year integrated, competency-based curriculum that by design offers students a faster pathway to graduation while protecting tuition revenues. This model significantly reduces delivery costs by integrating content and focusing on learning outcomes and the attainment of program competencies. Philosophically, the act of learning supersedes seat time. This model eliminates unnecessary redundancies within the curriculum, and it adds semester-ending credit bearing summative experiences. This model does more than rearrange existing curriculum; it leads to a complete redesign that enables institutions to pass along a 25 percent savings to students and their sponsors. It is a win-win for all concerned.

The integrated, competency-based model offers a legitimate response to the criticism of the continued high expenses of postsecondary education. Addressing the issue of cost while improving quality will prove to be the formula that saves many colleges and universities over the next several decades. But will institutional leaders be able to leave their comfort zones and challenge many of the basic assumptions that American higher education has held on to for so long? It seems to be clearer now than ever before that institutions need to embrace new practices or pay the ultimate price for their lack of will.

As the knowledge economy continues to rapidly expand, college graduates will need new skill sets in order to participate and successfully compete. Colleges and universities can and should play a central role in the preparation of citizens but only if the institutions have rethought the way that students acquire, tie together, and demonstrate new knowledge. Compartmentalized and silo-driven learning, so often redundant, is no longer meeting organizations' needs in today's global marketplace. The integrated, competency-based model that is discussed in detail in this book offers a proven approach that answers the growing chorus of concerns being expressed by business leaders, government officials, students, their sponsors, and academicians. The learning process can and must change in ways that improve its effectiveness while offering a clear solution to the continued escalating tuition crisis.

Three-Year Degrees in a Global Context

Today, there still remains substantial confusion as to what a three-year degree equals when comparing degree programs of various countries from around the world. For example, some believe that a three-year bachelor's program in the United States would be similar to degrees long offered in Europe and other countries globally. Although it is true that many Europeans can and do earn their bachelor's degree in three years, it is important to note that these students have participated in a system that requires thirteen years of elementary and secondary education: examples include the United Kingdom, Germany, and Italy. Indeed, in these instances the European model introduces students to many components of general education/liberal arts before they begin their bachelor's degree work. As a result, the bachelor's degree earned in Europe can be much more technical or professionally focused. Yet educators in the United Kingdom are quick to point out that the graduates of the system are equally if not better prepared for a well-rounded life, given the rigorous exit examination process that is required of all students.

In Europe today, forty-seven countries have agreed to the Bologna Process, a nongovernmental initiative designed to provide students with a more standardized or common educational experience (European Higher Education Area, 2011). One of the proposed benefits of the Bologna Process is to improve transferability of students' educational experiences across Europe. However, in some parts of Europe, students participate in a twelve-year elementary and secondary experience as opposed to the thirteen years of pre-university education. The harmonizing that is sought through the Bologna Process will be tested in these situations. Yet if the Bologna Process is successful, some have suggested that such a shift in educational strategy will assist Europe in regaining its educational might. In order to achieve the aims of the Bologna Process, countries will need to adopt common frameworks and measurable learning outcomes (Gaston, 2010).

In India, liberal arts degrees and courses receive less emphasis than subjects in technology, engineering, and business. Earning a bachelor's degree in technology or a bachelor's degree in engineering (both of which are four-year programs) provides students with a strong technical foundation. Students who then go on to earn an MBA from a different university compete strongly in the professional marketplace. Still, many three-year bachelor's degrees are available to students, such as the Bachelor of Commerce, Bachelor of Science, and Bachelor of Arts. However, U.S. institutions often require students with these degrees to complete an additional thirty credits of general education in order to earn a U.S. bachelor's degree.

The educational approach in India has been influenced by the rapid growth of that county's population. Because of the many thousands of outsourced jobs that have come to India from around the world, there is a premium on the development of technical skills and practical applications.

In Southeast Asia, the educational systems continue to show the influence of other nations: the British system in Malaysia, the French system in Vietnam, and the U.S. system in both Thailand and China. With that said, there remain fairly significant differences in the specific educational practices employed around the region. For example, outcomes assessment is not often used to demonstrate educational success. Rather, country-wide proficiency examinations have been used for decades in order to determine which students will have access to limited university educational opportunities. More recently, countries such as Thailand and China have placed greater emphasis on advancing their university-level educational systems in order to compete more effectively in the global economy.

Educational systems vary from country to country and have been developed and shaped over many decades by a multitude of factors including governmental structure, economic need, cultural norms, and political beliefs of the ruling party. What seems to be clearer today is that world leaders see the importance of strengthening regional educational systems in order to advance the opportunities that come with increased globalization. These proposed alliances have exciting possibilities, particularly with the Bologna process, given that one of its core focuses is on developing measurable outcomes. This approach will be discussed as this book examines the details of the integrated curriculum model and its reliance on competency demonstration (Keller, 2008; Wildavsky, 2010).

2

Core Components of Integrated
Three-Year Programs

The Accelerated Three-Year Model does not involve much, if any, curriculum reform. It relies primarily upon disciplined course scheduling, which may entail offering repeat sections of courses in order to meet the thirty-six-month graduation promise. The same can be said for the Prior Learning Model, depending upon how many course equivalents a student brings to the institution. These two three-year models may reduce tuition for students if they are not charged for the fourth year that they avoid. But neither model cuts institutional costs and may actually increase institutional delivery costs relative to revenue.

The Integrated Model, on the other hand, involves reworking the existing four-year curriculum, which can reduce institutional costs of course delivery and result in as much as 25 percent in tuition savings. A more complete explanation of the financial considerations can be found in Chapter 5.

This chapter discusses two of the three underlying core elements of integrated three-year programs: (1) the elimination of seat time as a primary measure of student learning and delivery of education and (2) the creation of a competency-based curriculum that focuses on measurable learning outcomes. It shows how program-level competencies lead to course-level academic plans that in turn facilitate program alignment and competency achievement. Chapter 3 will discuss the third core element, the design of educational experiences that align with program-level competencies. It will show how to rework existing four-year courses into three-year "modules." The processes described in these two chapters illustrate how to reduce traditional seat time to graduation as well as lower course-delivery costs to institutions. Chapter 6 will show ways to extend the classroom walls by utilizing virtual classroom environments as well as other important value-added dimensions of three-year models.

Integrated three-year programs are competency based and outcomes driven. They are six consecutive semesters in length without summer or weekend classes. The modules for the program's 120 credits can be team taught, cohort-based, interdisciplinary, and highly integrated, and they can deliver outcomes that are at least equal to a four-year program. With this model, institutions can cut delivery costs and pass along price savings to the students. Like the other three-year models, the Integrated Model can attract students who might not ordinarily attend the institution and help to ensure their retention.

Avoiding the Seat-Time Trap

Seat time continues to prevail in bachelor's degree education. Sometimes called "contact hours" or "class time," seat time is a convenient way for administrators to allocate and keep track of educational resources—professorial load, for example. Typically, students acquire the required 120 credit hours in forty three-credit courses or thirty four-credit courses that are evenly distributed over four years with summer and semester breaks. In this scenario, colleges offer fifteen-week semesters; in each semester there are forty contact hours per three-credit course times five courses equaling a total of 200 seat-time hours and fifteen credits. After eight such semesters, students graduate in four years with 120 credits amassed during 1,600 hours of seat time. That's assuming that nothing delays the students' progress and that they meet graduation requirements.

Of course, eight contiguous semesters is the ideal but is not always achieved. The national on-time bachelor's degree graduation rate in 2010 for four-year, "traditional"-selectivity, private institutions offering only bachelor's degrees is 34.5 percent. For public institutions with the same selectivity, it is 24.2 percent. The six-year graduation rate for traditional-selectivity private institutions is 45.2 percent, and for traditional-selectivity public schools, it is 45.1 percent (ACT, 2010a). These on-time graduation rates increase with selectivity. (Appendix B discusses sources of national graduation and retention statistics.)

But a bachelor's degree doesn't have to take four years. The U.S. Department of Education recognizes three-year bachelor's degrees: "An award (baccalaureate or equivalent degree, as determined by the Secretary, U.S. Department of Education) that normally requires at least four but not more than five years of full-time equivalent college-level work . . . also includes bachelor's degrees in which the normal four years of work are completed in three years" (NCES, 2010a). Furthermore, no higher-education-accrediting body actually requires 120 credits' worth of seat time for a bachelor's degree. In fact, the traditional bond between seat time and credit was broken with the advent of asynchronous online education, in which seat time is irrelevant and practically impossible to measure.

The New England Association of Schools and Colleges (NEASC) accredits 256 institutions of higher education in the United States. It recognizes that the connection between seat time and credit is not absolute and suggests "evidence-based and participatory inquiry" as a way to measure academic success. The association's policy on seat time reflects other U.S. regional accrediting bodies when it says that "in asynchronous programs the element of seat time is essentially removed from the equation. For these reasons, the institution conducts sustained, evidence-based and participatory inquiry as to whether distance learning programs are achieving objectives" (NEASC, 2010a, p. 14).

The NEASC policy of awarding academic credit indicates that seat time is only one component of time devoted to learning. NEASC explicitly recognizes out-of-class learning activities such as "preparation" and "asynchronous on-line learning." NEASC appears to be typical of U.S. regional accrediting bodies. This is NEASC's definition of a Unit of Credit:

> A quantification of student academic learning based on the amount of time a typical student spends engaged in academic study. One semester unit represents how much time a typical student is expected to devote to learning in one week of full time undergraduate study (at least 40–45 hours including, for example, class time and preparation or time engaged in asynchronous on-line learning). . . . A full-time undergraduate student program should normally be 14 to 16 units, and, if full time, no less than 12 units. (NEASC, 2010b, p. 2)

In *Educating Physicians: A Call for Reform of Medical School and Residency*, which consists of Carnegie Foundation–sponsored recommendations for medical education, Cooke and colleagues (2010) advocate for a move away from seat time in favor of a competency-based paradigm. Wellman and Ehrlich (2003a) explain how seat time and credit hours came to be so closely linked as the "most pervasive performance measure in higher education," and they appeal to institutions, federal and state agencies, and accreditation agencies to make "modest changes" (Wellman and Ehrlich, 2003b).

The recognition that higher-education-accrediting bodies and prestigious commissions have afforded to student learning outside the physical classroom, along with the use of evidence-based assessment, helps to break seat time's hold on higher education. This presents a golden opportunity to rework an existing four-year curriculum into three years without dilution of academic content or quality.

Competencies

In this book, the term "program-level competencies" refers to competencies that appear at several levels, including the institution, school, and academic major. These are competencies above course-level learning outcomes. Program-level competencies, along with their distribution and interconnections, are the building blocks for the Integrated Three-Year Model. Breaking seat-time constraints and creatively structuring learning experiences in support of program competencies can reduce the number of stand-alone courses required without diluting educational quality. These remaining "courses" are transformed into learning experiences called "modules" in three-year parlance. (This transformation is explored in Chapter 3.)

The competency-based movement in higher education has evolved to the point where many institutions adopt, adapt, or develop institution-level competencies for general education. An important example is from the Association of American Colleges and Universities. In addition, many schools or colleges within institutions and many programs within schools or colleges adopt, adapt, or develop their own competencies. Later in this chapter, Table 2.1 compares the AAC&U and the Southern New Hampshire University (SNHU) School of Business competencies.

Bloom, Hastings, and Madaus (1971), in the *Handbook on Formative and Summative Evaluation of Student Learning*, show that historically, the focus in program offerings has been on the "learning objectives." In contrast, Banta (2007a), in *Assessing Student Achievement in General Education*, explains how the competency-based education movement changed that focus. Learning objectives focus on what educators believe graduates should know, whereas competency-based education also focuses on what graduates need to be able to do in situations, complex and otherwise. According to the Council on Education for Public Health (CEPH, 2006), this is the difference between "teacher-focused" and "student and/or workplace focused" orientations.

There are several definitions of *competency*. Boyatzis (1982), in *The Competent Manager: A Model for Effective Performance*, says that a competency or skill is "the ability to demonstrate a system or sequence of behavior that is functionally related to attaining a performance goal" (p. 33). The Council on Education for Public Health (CEPH, 2006) says that competencies "state specifically what the student should expect to learn and be able to do upon completion of a program of study. This allows students to monitor their own progress and identify any gaps in skill attainment" (p. 5). Johnson and Johnson (1975), in *Joining Together: Group Theory and Group Skills*, define a competency as

> a system of behavior that can be applied in a wide range of situations. To become competent in any skill or knowledge area a person needs to understand the content both conceptually and behaviorally; have opportunities to practice it; get feedback on how well he or she is performing the skill or applying the knowledge; and use the competency often enough so that it is integrated into his or her behavioral repertoire. (p. 8)

In addition to Banta (2007a) and CEPH (2006), the Association of American Colleges and Universities (AAC&U, 2007) and Jones, Voorhees, and Paulson (2002) in *Defining and Assessing Learning: Exploring Competency-Based Initiatives* demonstrate that in competency-based education, the focus is on learning outcomes and their assessments. These in turn are often linked to employer needs as well as professional society guidelines. Identifying program competencies is a process that can lead faculty to rethink existing curricula content, sequence, and delivery. This is one way to successfully transform a four-year model into a three-year integrated model. Consider what the Council on Education for Public Health (CEPH, 2006) has to say about this process.

> Large skill sets are broken down into competencies, which may have sequential levels of mastery. Competencies reinforce one another from basic to advanced as learning progresses; the impact of increasing competencies is synergistic. . . . Competencies within different contexts may require different bundles of skills, knowledge and attitudes. The challenge is to determine which competencies can be bundled together to provide the optimal grouping for performing tasks. (p. 1)

Once program-level competencies have been established, learning experiences to support them need to be designed. Because many competencies are complex, learning experiences can often be designed from interdisciplinary perspectives, especially if cross-disciplinary teaching is encouraged. As Banta (2007a) points out, competencies are beneficial for faculty, students, and employers. Competencies help students understand what they are expected to know and be able to do, and they give educators a focus for instruction and assessment of learning outcomes. Competencies give employers a better feel than a simple transcript for what they can expect graduates to know and be able to do. Competency-based education benefits all stakeholders.

Program-Level Competencies

Program-level competencies are those designated by institutions (for example, general education requirements), schools within institutions (such as business schools or schools of arts and sciences), and three-year majors (for example, art, history, biology, business, computer science). Figure 2.1 illustrates the hierarchical relationships between competencies, learning experiences, and assessment

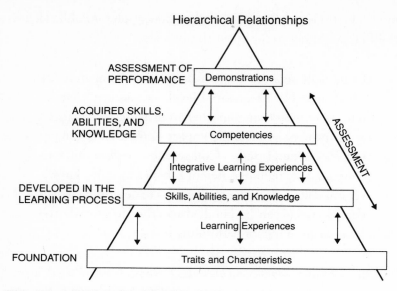

Figure 2.1. Hierarchical Relationships
   Source: E. Jones, R. Voorhees, and K. Paulson. (2002). *Defining and assessing learning: Exploring competency-based initiatives.* National Center for Education Statistics Publication: NCES 2002159, p. 8.

of student performance (Jones, Voorhees, & Paulson, 2002) and helps to explain how three-year curricula align with program-level competencies for maximum content coverage and efficient delivery of educational experiences. (Chapter 3 discusses academic plans, which are tools to ensure this alignment.)

   The bottom level in Figure 2.1 is the traits and characteristics that students bring to their education. The next level is the skills and abilities that students develop from particular learning experiences. The third level is the competencies, or the "skills, abilities and knowledge [that] interact to form bundles that have currency in relation to the task for which they were assembled." The competencies are achieved through integrative learning experiences. The top level is the result of applying competencies (Jones, Voorhees, & Paulson, 2002, p. 6). Notice that assessment is a part of each step in the hierarchy.

The relationship of course-level learning outcomes to program-level competencies is crucial. Learning experiences in particular modules produce measurable learning outcomes that align with program-level competencies (for example, academic major) that in turn align with higher program-level competencies (for example, school). This kind of alignment is the hallmark of an integrated three-year-degree program. It has been argued that competencies are a kind of covenant between students and their programs of study. As a technical assistance document from the Council on Education for Public Health (CEPH, 2006) points out, competencies "state specifically what the student should expect to learn and be able to do upon completion of a program of study. This allows students to monitor their own progress and identify any gaps in skill attainment" (p. 5). Competencies are a natural link between program goals and objectives in that they clearly specify what learners know and will be able to do in "varying and complex situations."

Thus, a set of agreed-upon competencies needs to be established for each degree program and also for the areas of specialization within programs. For example, a school of arts and sciences or a school of business might have a set of school-level competencies covering all of its academic majors. In addition, many professional societies publish guidelines that include program and even course competencies. For example, the Association of American Colleges and Universities (AAC&U, 2007) offers specific competencies, whereas the Association of Collegiate Business Schools and Programs (ACBSP, 2008) provides guidelines for developing these competencies. The Lumina Foundation for Education (2011) offers the *Degree Qualifications Profile* specifying learning outcomes that it sees as necessary to define quality in higher education.

Competencies and Their Associated Learning Experiences

For integrated three-year programs of study, the term *module* is used for what are typically called "courses" in four-year programs. Modules are more completely defined in a subsequent section.

Associated with these modules are learning outcomes, along with learning experiences (that is, activities that support the learning outcomes) that are clearly stated in the syllabus. These learning experiences, along with their associated assessment schemes, can be fully described in a module's academic plan. The plan helps instructors and administrators ensure that these learning experiences align with program competencies. Model syllabi are derived from academic plans, which are discussed in a subsequent section and treated in detail in Chapter 3.

Typically, an integrated program is a redesign of an existing eight-semester program so that it can be offered in just six semesters without diluting academic quality. Much has been written about curriculum design and redesign. Whether it be Diamond (2008) in *Designing and Assessing Courses and Curricula*, Lattuca and Stark (2009) in *Shaping the College Curriculum: Academic Plans in Context*, or Wolf and Hughes (2008) in *Curriculum Development in Higher Education: Faculty Driven Processes and Practices*, all agree that the key in this most important endeavor is keeping the focus upon goals, outcomes, and competencies and their relationships at all levels (that is, program and module). In this book, this is termed *alignment*. Once the four-year degree competencies and their relationships to learning outcomes and learning experiences have been identified, examined, and possibly revised, they can be distributed throughout a three-year curriculum (that is, the modules). This can lead to more effective and efficient ways to construct and deliver learning opportunities to students and for institutions. But only if they are properly aligned.

Of course, there is a strong need to assess demonstrations of competencies. Students bring a variety of traits and characteristics to the learning process and develop skills, abilities, and knowledge through learning experiences. In addition to modules, integrative learning experiences help to build and solidify competencies. This is the important third level in Figure 2.1. These kinds of integrative learning experiences play a prominent role in the construction of an integrated three-year-degree program. Deconstructing an existing four-year program into its various competencies, learning outcomes, and supporting learning experiences precedes the efforts to rebuild it into a three-year integrated program.

Redesigning the Curriculum

One way to gain effectiveness and efficiencies in three-year-program delivery is to eliminate unnecessary redundancies that exist in the established four-year curriculum while maintaining 120 credits of content, the agreed-upon competencies, and streamlining the learning process. Some competencies and their supporting activities can be moved outside their existing four-year courses into other existing courses. When the entire set of competencies in a particular course is spread throughout other courses, that particular course is no longer needed in the curriculum. This reduces the number of courses that the institution needs to deliver for a particular program, which in turn reduces the overall delivery costs, further increasing institution efficiency. This is the institutional "win" part of the "win-win" associated with the Integrated Three-Year Model. Redistributing competencies without reducing academic quality is the challenge. This is why a competency-based approach with its reliance on identifiable learning goals and outcomes, along with their monitoring and assessment, is so important.

In order to realize these efficiencies, the program-level competencies need to be determined. Mapping where and when these competencies are addressed in each of the courses that constitute the existing four-year degree is a crucial endeavor. Also, course-level outcomes need to be determined. To do this, the following information is needed: (1) where topics and skills and their associated learning activities appear and are sequenced in the program of study; (2) whether these topics and skills are foundational, reinforcing, or contributory; (3) whether their level of emphasis is high, medium, or low; and (4) what program-level competencies they support. Alignment of course learning outcomes and program-level competencies is crucial to maintain the integrity of the emerging three-year program with respect to the existing four-year program.

Educational experiences and their learning outcomes support competencies in different ways. Intentional learning experiences provided at the introductory level are foundational (F). When a competency has been introduced and the object is to reinforce it, learning experiences are reinforcing (R). Or learning experiences that support the development of competencies but are not necessary for competency development are described as contributory (C). In other words, they are prior to a foundation.

In addition, educational experiences can have different levels of emphasis. The emphasis can be characterized as high (H), meaning that it is crucial to the module. When the emphasis is moderate (M), the topic area requires substantial attention in the delivery of the educational experience and content. When the emphasis is low (L), the topic area has a minimal relationship in the module's overall impact on the student.

Determining Program-Level Competencies

Many professional societies, in concert with employers, already have developed competencies for programs in their areas. These competencies can be adopted whole-cloth or partially, or they can be modified. Where program-level competencies do not already exist, educators can develop them. The Association of American Colleges and Universities Essential Learning Outcomes (AAC&U, 2007) and the Southern New Hampshire University (SNHU) School of Business competencies (SNHU School of Business, 2011) are two examples of program-level competencies; they are shown in Table 2.1. It would be a valuable exercise for the leaders of any institution to see how their program-level competencies match up with national and professional society standards.

No matter how they are determined, program-level competencies are the building blocks for the transformation of a four-year

Table 2.1. Association of American Colleges and Universities (AAC&U) Essential Learning Outcomes and Southern New Hampshire University (SNHU) School of Business Competencies

AAC&U Essential Learning Outcomes	SNHU School of Business Competencies
Knowledge of human cultures and the physical and natural world • Through study in the sciences and mathematics, social sciences, humanities, histories, languages, and the arts *Focused by engagement with big questions, both contemporary and enduring* **Intellectual and practical skills, including** • Inquiry and analysis • Critical and creative thinking • Written and oral communication • Quantitative literacy • Information literacy • Teamwork and problem solving *Practiced extensively, across the curriculum, in the context of progressively more challenging problems, projects, and standards for performance*	1. **Communication:** Students will demonstrate an ability to communicate effectively through written, oral, and other forms of communication. 2. **Information Technology:** Students will master information technology principles and contemporary information technology applications and will be able to apply information technology to the greatest advantage in the many aspects of an organization's operations. 3. **Problem Solving:** Students will develop the skills to identify problems quickly, analyze them reasonably, and find solutions creatively. 4. **Teamwork:** Students will develop a broad range of interpersonal skills in order to function effectively as a participant in team and group situations. 5. **Analytical Skills:** Students will appropriately use and apply quantitative and qualitative methods of analysis, use data, applied mathematical and statistical techniques, and decision sciences whenever possible to attain organizational objectives.

(continued)

Table 2.1. (Continued)

AAC&U Essential Learning Outcomes	SNHU School of Business Competencies
Personal and social responsibility, including • Civic knowledge and engagement—local and global • Intercultural knowledge and competence • Ethical reasoning and action • Foundations and skills for lifelong learning *Anchored through active involvement with diverse communities and real-world challenges* **Integrative and applied learning, including** • Synthesis and advanced accomplishment across general and specialized studies *Demonstrated through the application of knowledge, skills, and responsibilities to new settings and complex problems*	6. **Global Orientation:** Students will attain a multidisciplinary global perspective order to understand others and make more effective international business decisions. 7. **Legal and Ethical Practices:** Students will realize the legal and ethical considerations and implications of personal, social, business and international business behavior and activities. 8. **Research:** Students will be able to conduct primary and secondary research and apply the results for informed decision-making. 9. **Strategic Approach:** Students will be able to think and plan strategically in making business decisions. 10. **Leadership:** Students will be able to function effectively as a team and organizational leader.
AAC&U. (2007). Essential learning outcomes. *College learning for the new global century: A report from the National Leadership Council for Liberal Education and America's Promise* (p. 12). Washington, DC: AAC&U. Retrieved from http://www.uwyo.edu/accreditation/_files/docs/Essential_Learning_Outcomes.pdf	Southern New Hampshire University School of Business. (2011). *Business competencies.* Retrieved from http://www.snhu.edu/361.asp

program into a three-year program. Program-level competencies come first. Chapter 3 describes one such endeavor as well as the crucial alignment between these competencies and course learning outcomes.

Analyzing Course-Level Learning Outcomes

The determination of module-level learning outcomes is a necessary big step in moving from a four-year to a three-year integrated model. This involves course-level data collection and analyses. Whether or not a competency-based curriculum is already present, all existing courses in the traditional four-year major need close scrutiny because aligning course-level learning outcomes with program-level competencies is a key activity and it needs to be done right. This entails agreement among faculty about what aspects of the curriculum should be taught, especially in major courses, as well as a detailed description of all academic experiences. Where course-level learning outcomes already exist, they need to be examined to determine not only how they align with program-level competencies but also where they are foundational, reinforced, and contributory throughout the curriculum as well as what their levels of intensity are.

Course-level learning outcomes must be examined in order to eliminate unnecessary redundancies and relocate some learning outcomes and their associated learning activities to different courses. For example, one such examination revealed that theories of motivation appeared in seven different courses at the foundational (F) level and that some of these courses were requisites for the others. Faculty experts concluded that adjustments were necessary. Also, depending upon the results of the analyses, faculty can consider combining multicourse learning outcomes into new courses.

Where course-level learning outcomes do not already explicitly exist, faculty will want to note which existing courses and credits are needed to satisfy the major area. Also, they will need to identify

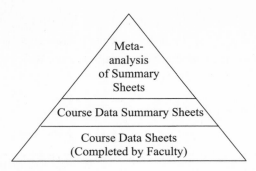

Figure 2.2. Data Collection and Analysis Pyramid

which courses and how many credits in the university core are needed. The same goes for school core courses and any allied courses in the existing four-year program. Then, faculty members who teach these courses can be surveyed in order to develop matrices of course topics or learning outcomes versus program-level competencies for each existing course as suggested by Banta (2007b) in *Assessing Student Learning in the Disciplines*. This is the first step in the three-step process shown in Figure 2.2.

Figure 2.3 is a sample of a form for information collected in the bottom level of the Figure 2.2 pyramid. It is a partial example matrix completed by faculty teaching a single four-year curriculum course where individual course topics or learning outcomes address program-level competencies. The rows in Figure 2.3 are the identified topics or learning outcomes in the course. The columns are the program-level competencies. The letters in the cells at the row-column intersections indicate the level of emphasis (high [H], moderate [M], low [L]), which calls for the professional judgment of the content expert, and whether the course topic establishes the foundation (F) upon which the program-level competency is achieved, reinforces (R) the program-level competency that was already established, or contributes (C) to the program-level competency prior to a foundation. The full table is shown in Appendix 1 at http://www.josseybass.com/go/martinbradley.

COURSE NO: _____	COURSE TITLE: _____				Prepared by: _____		
COURSE TOPICS/LEARNING OUTCOMES	Competencies						
	Communication	Info Tech	Problem Solving	Teamwork	Analytical Skills	Global Orientation	Leg: Eth Prac
Operation Management	H-F		M-R				M-
Organizational Behavior				M-F		M-F	
Marketing		H-F		M-R		H-F	
Accounting	L-R		M-R	M-F	L-C	M-R	H-

H	- High Emphasis Area - Crucial to the nature of the course.
M	- Moderate Emphasis Area - A topic area that requires substantial attention in the delivery of course content.
L	- Low Emphasis Area - A topic area that has a minimal relationship in the overall impact of the course on the student.

C	- This course supports the development of competencies when they occur but is not a necessary condition for competency development. In o
F	- This course establishes the Foundation upon which the skill or knowledge is achieved.
R	- This course Reinforces the skill or knowledge, important to the achievement of the common professional component.

Figure 2.3. Sample Data-Collection Course Form—Course Topics/ Learning Outcomes by Program-Level Competencies

Looking at Figure 2.3, you can see that the course-content expert believes that accounting topics, or learning outcomes, reinforce (R) the program-level competency Problem Solving with medium (M) intensity. These same accounting topics are also contributory (C) with low (L) emphasis for the Analytical Skills program-level competency.

Consider an example with a different program-level competency set. The topic of Greek philosophy in Introduction to Humanities, may serve as a foundation for the general education program-level competencies of Creative and Innovative Thinking and Problem Analysis while at the same time be reinforcing for the program-level competencies of Reading Competence and Aesthetic Appreciation.

After the content and discipline experts complete individual course data sheets, the next step is to summarize the data as a frequency count over all courses with respect to the program-level competencies. An example summary table is shown in Table 2.2. The full table with an explanation on how to construct it is provided in Appendix 2 at http://www.josseybass.com/go/martinbradley. Notice how this tabulation can show gaps in coverage, which may or

Table 2.2. Sample Tabulation of Topics/Learning Outcomes by Course and Program Competencies

																Competencies
	Communication			Info Tech			Problem Solving			Teamwork			Analytical Skills			C Ori
	1			2			3			4			5			
Course	F	R	C	F	R	C	F	R	C	F	R	C	F	R	C	F
BUS 201	7	3					9	2					10	1		
BUS 202	2	9	4	2	3		4	12					3	10	2	10
BUS 206	1			5												5
BUS 210		6		4				10						11		3
BUS 211		9		4				10						11		3
BUS 320		3		3	7		12	7		4			13	6		5
BUS 333	3	2		2			2	4						2		3
BUS 350	1	1		3	2		3			10			3			3
BUS 375	1	2		3	8		1							2		
BUS 408	7	13			1		6	8		10	9					
BUS 421	2	4	12		2	1	6	13	8	13	8	6	2	15	14	5
Total	24	52	16	26	23	1	43	66	8	37	17	6	31	58	16	37

may not be important. The bottom-line totals may also alert faculty to possible unnecessary redundancies.

For example, the tabulation of competencies in Table 2.2 shows that the school-level Problem Solving competency was addressed forty-three times in a foundational manner over the program courses. This result might signal unnecessary redundancies. Suppose that the school-level Teamwork competency is reinforced seventeen times—all in only two of the program courses. This may indicate that Teamwork reinforcement needs to be spread through more of the program's curriculum. At this point, the results of the analyses can be returned to the content specialist and the sponsoring department for a reality check that might warrant another iteration of data collection. Analyses like these can be very revealing and help curriculum developers understand the distribution and types of relationships between course-level learning outcomes and program-level competencies.

In the first step, data is collected on all four-year courses. An illustrative example is shown in Figure 2.3. In the second step, these data can be compiled into course data summary sheets as shown in Table 2.2. The third step is a comprehensive, multidimensional meta-analysis to more readily identify what and where unnecessary redundancies and overlaps exist. This meta-analysis, the top of the pyramid in Figure 2.2, also helps to identify what and where foundational material is or is not built upon in the existing program. A partial meta-analysis grid is shown in Table 2.3. Notice that the frequency data are shown by competency and other pertinent categories. The full table and how to construct it is in Appendix 3 at http://www.josseybass.com/go/martinbradley.

The second column in Table 2.3 indicates the number of courses supporting the particular program-level competencies. In this example, school-level competencies are the rows, and the third column shows the number of course topics or learning outcomes that are foundational, reinforcing, and contributory for each of the competencies. This data is broken down further into specific course learning experiences (that is, columns four and up) with their particular counts against program-level competencies. In this particular example, course levels (such as 200-level courses) are as granular as it gets. Understanding what topics and learning experiences occur in which courses and how they are related to program competencies is crucial to converting topics into learning outcomes, creating and sequencing three-year modules, and making transparent the relational structure of the program.

Recap

This chapter focused on rejecting the seat-time trap in order to create a competency and learning-outcomes-based curriculum to achieve program-level competencies in six semesters and 120 credits without students having to resort to extra semester, summer, or weekend courses. In order to transition from a four-year program to a three-year program, it is necessary to deconstruct the former. One way to do this is to identify program-level competencies and

Table 2.3. Sample Meta-analysis of Course Topics/Learning Outcomes by Program Competencies and Distribution

COMPETENCY	# OF COURSES SUPPORTING	TOTAL # OF C/F/R	No. of C, F, R by course level (Freshmen-100, Sophomore-200, Junior-300, Senior-400)											
			C&100	C&200	C&300	C&400	F&100	F&200	F&300	F&400	R&100	R&200	R&300	R&400
Communication	13 of 17	C=6, F=2, R=7	3	3	0	0	1	1	0	0	5	2	0	0
Information Technology	15 of 17	C=11, F=0, R=5	8	3	0	0	0	0	0	0	0	3	2	0
Problem Solving	6 of 17	C=6, F=0, R=1	4	2	1	0	0	0	0	0	1	0	0	0

collect course-level data on learning experiences and outcomes as they support competency achievement. The subsequent meta-analyses help track the learning activities and outcomes over courses that may contain unnecessary redundancies and that could indicate opportunities to spread these activities and learning outcomes over existing courses or into new courses. Creating three-year modules along with their sequencing and relationships to such things as inter- and intra-module themes are taken up in Chapter 3.

3

Curriculum Reformulation
Courses into Modules

The three-stage analyses of course-content learning outcomes and their relationships to program-level competencies, which were shown in Chapter 2, set the stage for reformatting and reformulating the existing curriculum. These analyses can ascertain whether and where learning outcomes and the corresponding learning experiences can best be sequenced in the curriculum. They show where adjustments can be made and where the total number of four-year courses might be reduced while addressing the requisite competencies in a manner that preserves the program's academic quality. Walvoord (2010), in *Assessment Clear and Simple: A Practical Guide for Institutions, Departments, and General Education*, provides guidance and the details involved in reformatting and reformulating curricula.

An example of one such adjustment from the Southern New Hampshire University (SNHU) experience has to do with a three-credit public speaking course required in the four-year program. One consequence of the three-stage analyses was that its competencies were distributed throughout a number of integrated three-year modules and end-of-semester integrating experiences, both explained below. Thus, a separate public speaking module was not needed in the three-year program. That's one less course or module to deliver. Hypothetically, the same case might be made for distributing elementary mathematics topics throughout an existing information technology course (or vice versa), thus eliminating another course or module from the curriculum yet ensuring that the competencies would be achieved elsewhere.

Module Design

As a result of the three-stage competency analyses, the four-year curriculum can be reconstituted into three-year modules with optional submodules. A module can stand alone or can be conceptualized as being composed of two or more submodules. For example, a communications module may be designed to span an entire semester but be broken up into a six-week composition submodule and a nine-week literature submodule. The submodules would be interrelated with overarching module themes. There might also be overarching semester themes that relate to all modules, as shown in Figure 3.1. (Themes are also covered in Chapter 6.)

A module is one or more associated academic areas of study that can be logically grouped together. A module could also be composed of less directly related areas of study grouped under a theme to achieve the desired learning outcomes and competencies. An example is the end-of-semester integrating experience. This experience is shown in Figure 3.1 and will be discussed later in this chapter.

There is a high degree of coordination between academic areas within a module in order to (1) achieve rapid cognitive mastery, (2) achieve a high level of mutually reinforcing, goal-oriented activities, (3) provide foundational and building activities for the competencies, while reducing the number of multiple and unnecessary initiating activities, (4) eliminate unnecessary overlap and redundancy, (5) create an environment in which course-equivalent activities can be conducted, (6) establish academic threads within a module within a year, (7) ensure that modules are guided by their themes, and (8) ensure that modules are rooted in quality.

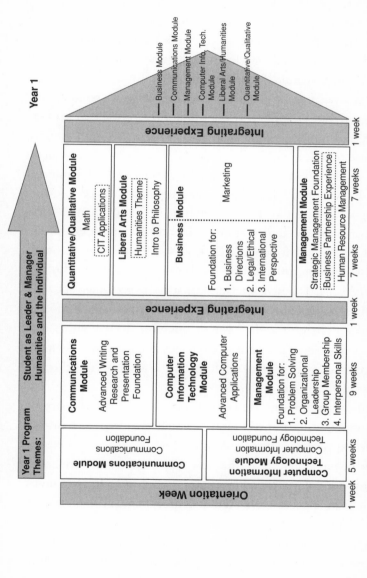

Figure 3.1. Year-One Modules, Themes, and Integrating Experiences

There is also a high degree of cooperation between module instructors and thus coordination between modules within a year (that is, intra-year) in order to achieve goals 1–8 and to (9) facilitate the development of cognitive mastery and skill demonstration between modules, (10) contribute to the integrated and holistic nature of the academic experience for the students and the instructors, (11) establish academic linkages between the modules, and (12) minimize academic discontinuities.

And finally, there is also coordination between modules between years (that is, inter-year coordination) in order to achieve goals 1–8 and to (13) ensure that multiyear themes are followed, (14) ensure that academic linkages and continuity are maintained between years, and (15) create a holistic, integrated academic experience between years in a three-year program.

In Figure 3.1, notice the overarching yearlong theme, "Student as leader and manager/Humanities and the individual," and the two Computer Information Technology submodules that constitute a Computer Information Technology module in the first semester. Also, a Management module spans both semesters, with Management submodules located in each semester. Each module could have a theme for the year or semester. It is notable that the end-of-semester integrating experience is itself a module made up of indirectly related areas of study that are connected through integrative educational activities.

Recall that the term *module* is being used instead of *course* in order to make a sharp distinction between the original four-year academic experiences (that is, courses) and the three-year-degree academic experiences. It is the learning experiences associated with these modules that address topics and learning outcomes, which in turn support competency achievement. The idea is to construct learning experiences that support course-level learning outcomes, which in turn align with program-level competencies. And in order to offer a credible integrated three-year program, these learning experiences need to be delivered in six semesters without summers or weekends and without any dilution of academic quality. There is more about the character of these learning experiences in Chapter 6.

Levels and Sequences

It is one thing to create a list of course-level learning outcomes in a program of study, but it is quite another thing to identify their particular levels and necessary sequences within the program. These things influence the mix of the academic experiences (that is, modules and submodules) that must be constructed next.

Three-year-degree modules need to address all the agreed-upon content and learning outcomes without containing unnecessary redundancies. The modules need to be specifically designed to contribute to program-level competency achievement. Ideally, each module and submodule is, by design, inextricably linked to all of the others through mutually reinforcing intramodular and intermodular learning experiences. Cross-disciplinary pollination and coordination are module and program hallmarks.

Figure 3.2 is a business administration example of how individual modules in a program of study are related to program competencies. The letters in small circles in the figure represent the program-level competencies. In this example, the competencies addressed in the first Computer Information Technology submodule are also addressed in the first Communications submodule. This intentional design is representative of the cross-disciplinary nature of the curriculum.

In addition, year-one modules can be sequenced to provide students with the foundations for competencies during the first part of the academic year. Then, these competencies can be built upon and reinforced in the second part of year one and throughout years two and three. All submodules are explicitly linked to various program-level competencies. Competency development and reinforcement occur at varying levels of intensity in each of the modules and are

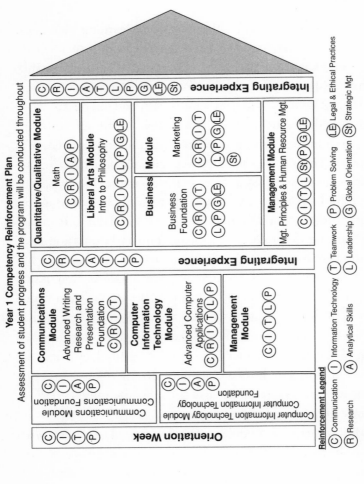

Figure 3.2. Program Competency Reinforcement Plan, Business Administration Example

coordinated and planned through a comprehensive master planning document to ensure competency alignment. It is these academic plans, which will be discussed later in this chapter, that ensure cross-curricular support of competencies throughout all three years of the program.

Integrating Academic Experiences

We have already shown how sets of learning experiences and learning outcomes from existing four-year courses can be gathered together to create a new module, thus eliminating some of the existing courses and saving institutional delivery costs.

There are other ways to create academic experiences that, although not traditional modules derived from four-year courses, still offer significant academic content and credits to students. One way is to create a space during semesters for students to participate in intensive synthesizing study and work that not only reinforce previously learned material and processes but also integrate new learning materials and processes. Here, competencies can be reinforced, expanded, and reflected upon in a multitude of innovative and diverse academic experiences, such as the creation and management of a consulting activity or major group project during the entirety of year three as well as the weeklong integrating experiences during the last week of each semester in years one and two.

End-of-semester and yearlong integrating experiences are curriculum innovations that can be built into the Integrated Three-Year-Degree Model. They can account for earned credits that in turn help not only to make the Integrated Model truly integrative but also to save the institution course-delivery costs because these experiences can be staffed by module instructors at little or no additional cost.

Experience shows that group-oriented integrating experiences in business, such as case studies and work for for-profit and nonprofit organizations, provide beneficial challenges for students. Would the same kind of group-oriented activity also be applicable to a discipline in the liberal arts? Would an integrating experience be appropriate, for example, for the study of literature?

At its basis, the art of literature is meant to be experienced on a personal level. English teachers strive to help their students, at whatever level in the educational system, develop an appreciation and even a love of literature in its many genres. In an integrating experience in literature, faculty members could assign students a project, such as the development of a study guide, that would help others gain a full appreciation of a literary artist. They might, for example, select a contemporary poet and ask students to use all they have previously learned about meter, rhyme, imagery, and tone to help others appreciate that poet's work. Or faculty might select a novelist and ask students to prepare a study guide to use what they have learned about plot, theme, character development, and mood to help others appreciate that novelist's work and motivate them to explore other novels by other authors. Students would be expected not only to use what they have learned but also to push beyond their knowledge boundaries to learn more. Another integrating experience in literature could consist of the group development of a publishable paper that applies writings in literary criticism to a specific literary artist or a literary movement. The goal, therefore, in any integrating experience in literature would be for students to enhance their own understanding of literature and to increase the appreciation of others for an art that can enrich their lives.

End-of-Semester Weeklong Integrating Experiences

An integrating experience can be placed after the conclusion of the modules in each of the first four semesters in the three-year-degree program. It can be considered as a module in and of itself. This configuration is shown in Figures 3.1 and 3.2. As part of the three-year-degree curriculum design, faculty can create a space within the traditional semester wherein students are required and challenged to demonstrate the integration of theories and concepts from their previous weeks of study. These one-week integrating experiences are carefully designed to help students synthesize course material, reinforce knowledge and skills, and understand the relevance and relatedness of their studies in the program. They are also designed to introduce new material. The experiences could consist of case studies completed by student teams or some other type of project.

An example is a case study about art furniture by three-year-degree students in business administration. After a semester that included module work in a number of disciplines including ethics, humanities, accounting, and economics, the students were given a comprehensive case for the semester-ending integration project. The case focused on the art furniture world. In order for the students to successfully complete the case, they needed to apply concepts taught and skills developed in previously completed modules.

Because the students had never been exposed to the art furniture industry, they had to research and learn about art furniture as a market in the United States. They had to appreciate and understand the challenges of doing business globally as well as understand the intricacies of running an import business. One requirement was that students had to teach their grading faculty about art furniture and the growing role of art furniture in the United States.

The U.S. dealer in the case study sought to be the exclusive dealer of high-end European art furniture. The furniture pieces typically sold for $2,000 up to $50,000. This case study required students to extend their knowledge of humanities, economics, accounting, ethics, and business management while expanding their understanding of how the whole of what they were learning in their curriculum was much greater than the sum of its parts. It also required that they effectively communicate their findings through a formal oral presentation to their grading faculty and the submission of a written document.

In these integrating experiences, students are placed in work teams by their teaching faculty. The teams are designed to be as heterogeneous as possible. Gordon (2001) in *Organizational*

Behavior and Katzenbach and Smith (1993) in *The Wisdom of Teams* show that heterogeneous teams, although more challenging in the early stages of development, do in fact lead to higher degrees of creativity than homogeneous teams achieve.

The integrating experience can be organized as an intense seven-day academic activity that begins with a kickoff meeting during which students receive instructions about team makeup and what is required over the next seven days for the case or problem set. The integrating experience serves several academic purposes: It reinforces many of the program competencies such as, for example, teamwork, interpersonal communication, communications, information technology, and problem solving. It demonstrates students' acquisition and integration of new knowledge, and it serves as a capstone experience for the just-completed semester of learning. In years one and two, student teams can get a comprehensive case that is often drawn from real-world events from the previous year. During this weeklong integrating experience, students are required to demonstrate that they have met the minimum standard of work duration commensurate with the number of academic credits involved. Their work can consist of individual study, research, and writing in addition to collaborative teamwork.

The integrating experience provides students with the opportunity to demonstrate to their faculty and other members of the university community the knowledge, skills, and abilities that they acquired and developed throughout the semester in addition to new material that they learned during the integrating experience. The teaching faculty may intentionally select activities to build on the yearly themes (discussed in Chapter 6) or material from the recently completed modules as well as to extend students' learning in new ways. There can be a number of very specific requirements that reinforce the competencies and learning outcomes of the three-year-degree curriculum and stretch the students to learn new material. During the weeklong experience, teams research the case or project and design a multimedia presentation to present to the faculty that addresses the charges given to them on the first day. During the week, faculty members act as consultants to the teams and are available to meet with them both face to face and through a virtual collaborative environment.

On the last day, teams present their findings to their teaching faculty and other invited members of the university community. Members of other teams do not attend the presentations. This is consistent with the notion that a primary goal of the integrating experience is not competition between teams but rather a focus on a standard of excellence within one's own team. Students earn academic credit toward their 120-credit overall total. Shortly after the integrating experience, students receive a detailed narrative evaluation from their grading faculty. As designed, the integrating experience lends itself to a team-based grading schema. Thus, although students receive individual and team feedback, teams receive a common grade. Students are required to complete 360° evaluations and, if through the assessment process someone is identified as a low contributor or a noncontributor, then that student's individual grade could be adjusted based on further investigation by the grading faculty. The peer-based assessment framework is discussed in Chapter 6.

As part of faculty members' commitment to the program, they participate in the selection of integrating content and assess student performance. When the integrating experience is not seen as part of a faculty member's teaching responsibilities for their respective module, additional compensation may be appropriate.

Yearlong Integrating Experience

In year three of the three-year program, students can join together and operate as an organizational entity for the purposes of providing a service to area, regional, or national enterprises. The integrating experience is comprehensive and all-encompassing for the students. It extends over the entire third year and, depending on design, it is the equivalent of one or more credit-bearing modules. This experience can be viewed as a yearlong senior project. For example, creative writing majors could run a literary magazine or perform outreach to help needy children appreciate the joys writing and of good literature. Because an integrated three-year program operates well with a cohort of students and because these students are used to participating in intact workgroups by year three, it is relatively easy to create an opportunity that places them in an environment where they must identify, contact, and market their services to a deserving local or distant enterprise. Naturally, this is done under faculty supervision, guidance, and assessment.

The transformative nature of such an experience should not be underestimated. When the yearlong integrating experience is done right, students have greatly matured by the end of the school year and are almost uniformly ready to enter the workforce in highly productive roles or to go on to graduate school ready to excel.

In *The Degree Qualifications Profile*, the Lumina Foundation for Education (2011) advances "applied learning" as one of five basic learning areas. Its description is exactly what the yearlong integrating experience is about:

> The Applied Learning outcomes make it clear that, beyond what graduates know, what they can *do* with what they know is the ultimate benchmark of learning. They emphasize a commitment to analytic inquiry, active learning, real-world problem solving, and innovation—all of which are vital in today's evolving workplace and in society. Applied Learning should be viewed as a core element of the student experience. (p. 8)

In the fall semester, the senior class with their instructor's guidance develops a vision, mission, business strategies, and other components of a business plan that they will use to carry out their project activities throughout the academic year. During this yearlong integrating experience, students develop organizational policies and employment contracts that define the roles and responsibilities they accept as participants in the integrating experience. Having a business-faculty member as part of the year-three integrating-experience faculty team can be very helpful.

Each senior class, in consultation with their faculty, is encouraged to take the project in a direction that best fits the skill area and talents of the group. As in the case of the year-one and year-two integrating experiences, the seniors are required to make end-of-semester presentations to their "clients"—their faculty and the community. The content of these presentations focuses on the business plan, key business strategies, operational issues, and the evaluation of deliverables that the students provided to the clients. Typically, the cohort is divided into teams to take on different clients. Evaluation procedures similar to years one and two are used to assign grades and award credits to the students.

Examples of Yearlong Integrating-Experience Projects

Manchester, NH, Community Health Center (2004)

> The student team researched and analyzed the 340B prescription drug plan offered by U.S. government to qualifying agencies. The research and analysis was based on predetermined criteria that identified the benefits of the 340B plan versus one of the current drug discount plans utilized by the Manchester Community Health Center.

American Express Financial Advisors (2005)

> This group needed to improve business development and client retention through a series of marketing events. Branding the corporate image and supporting the local community were key factors when determining the focus of each event. The student team analyzed the strategic benefits and costs associated with the four recommended events, which served to enhance client relations and branding.

New Hampshire Supreme Court Society (2010)

> The project focused on research, data collection, process documentation, and development of a standard-operating-procedure manual about the appropriate practices and protocol for archiving court-related documents. An associated training manual was created to ensure each new volunteer would be adequately prepared for his or her respective internship.

For a more complete list spanning many years, see Appendix 4: Examples of SNHU Yearlong Integrating-Experience Projects at http://www.josseybass.com/go/martinbradley.

The yearlong integrating experience can be a very powerful and comprehensive learning experience for the students. They get to experience firsthand the benefits and practical applications of their curriculum. The curriculum takes on life and becomes meaningful for them. The integrating experience can also provide a forum for faculty and students to share, discuss, debate, and advance the understanding of the challenges that the participants face. Faculty involvement in the integrating experience can lead to collaborative conversations across disciplines, and like the end-of-semester integrating experiences, students earn academic credit for something beyond a standard three-year module. The value to future employers of students who have had this real-world consulting experience is extraordinary.

Academic Plans

Module-based academic planning documents are crucial for quality control and transparency for any three-year curriculum. They address the needs of instructors, administrators, and accrediting bodies. Academic plans can help ensure alignments between program-level competencies and module-level learning outcomes. The plans map module topics and learning experiences to their module-level learning outcomes and then to program-level competencies. When carefully coordinated, academic plans provide a powerful means of formative assessment.

In addition, the academic plan associates module-level assessment processes with each competency. This is crucial for substantiating the progress of individual students in module learning outcomes and program-level competency. In addition, it gives instructors a valuable road map for understanding the relationships between their module and those of other instructors and with program-level competencies. Figure 3.3 illustrates the alignment relationships.

An academic plan is much more than a syllabus. A plan first lists the specific program competencies that the module addresses. Next, the plan identifies module-level learning outcomes, and for each one it lists the implementing activities that address the specific program competency. Learning activities, called "implementing activities" in the academic plan, can be categorized as foundational,

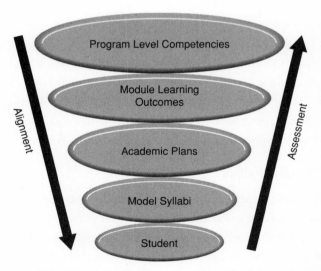

Figure 3.3. Alignment and Assessment Relationships for Academic Plans

reinforcing, and contributing, as Chapter 2 explained. A fully developed academic plan for a Communications module is provided in Appendix C. Academic plans are typically in three parts.

Part one of an academic plan identifies modules and any submodules that run concurrently. This gives instructors a sense of what students are learning contemporaneously. Recall that student cohorts are preferred so that students in, for example, year one take the same modules. There are many advantages to this kind of learning community. If a module is composed of submodules, then any linking themes between them are easily presented to the students. Any linking themes for modules running concurrently are likewise revealed. Themes and learning communities are discussed in Chapter 6.

Part two of an academic plan describes the overall semester strategy with respect to competencies in the various modules whether or not they are running concurrently. This is a way for all concerned—students, teachers, and administrators—to gain the big academic picture.

Part three is all about identifying learning goals, which typically appear on a module syllabus, and the learning activities that are associated with these goals and specific program-level competencies. These module-level learning activities are further identified as being foundational for a competency or competencies, reinforcing, or contributory. Assessment modalities are also included with each implementing activity. An example of an academic plan for a three-year Management module can be found in Appendix D.

Model Module Syllabi

A model syllabus is meant to guide module instructors with respect to content coverage and sequence. It derives directly from a corresponding academic plan. A model syllabus would thus be offered to module instructors to show how to carry out the academic plan. It is intended to ensure quality control while allowing the instructor to exercise academic freedom. There is an example model syllabus in Appendix E that is associated with the model academic plan in Appendix D.

Module Mappings into Four-Year Courses

Assuming that a three-year program runs alongside an existing four-year program, some provision needs to be made for modules in year one to correspond to existing courses in the traditional four-year program. This mapping facilitates credit transfer should a student leave the three-year-degree program in either of the year-one semesters and provides an accounting for the blending of former course learning outcomes across modules. There has been a previous discussion about how to transform a four-year eight-semester model into a three-year integrated model by identifying program-level competencies, rearranging and/or distributing learning outcomes throughout modules, and introducing integrating experiences into the program. End-of-semester integrating experiences may map into existing four-year courses, but they might also map into electives or designated independent studies.

Recap

Creating three-year modules involves collection and analyses of data and the design of learning experiences that develop and support module-level learning outcomes, which in turn support program-level competencies. Alignment between learning outcomes and program-level competencies is key in assuring that academic quality is maintained. Many of these learning experiences will already be in place in four-year courses that can be turned into three-year modules. But at this level of detail, it is important not only to reexamine existing learning experiences but to be sure that they are sequenced correctly for maximum student learning. Three-year modules need to map back to four-year courses for verification of content addressed and credits earned.

Designing three-year modules is a golden opportunity for subject matter experts to work together across disciplines to present material that helps students see that disciplinary boundaries can sometimes be somewhat arbitrary. Leveraging academic content in this way is one of the value-added dimensions that will be discussed in Chapter 6, that is, professional learning communities where educators play a crucial role in developing the three-year competency-based degree. As Chapter 4 will show, faculty buy-in and sustained participation are crucial in order to transform a four-year degree into a three-year-degree program.

4

The Case for an Integrated Three-Year Model

As discussed in Chapter 1, an integrated, competency-based three-year-degree model is a significant departure from the traditional four-year baccalaureate-degree program and involves much more than simply accelerating the speed of degree completion. This effort requires a significant restructuring of the undergraduate curriculum. Although 120 credits are still required for graduation, with this new model, academic leaders are challenged to think differently about how to organize and deliver the academic content for these credits so that the degree program can be completed in three years without requiring students to take courses at night, on weekends, or during the summer months and/or intersessions. In the Integrated Model, model syllabi, academic planning documents, interdisciplinary collaboration among the teaching faculty, integration of module content, and the focus on demonstration of program competencies as the means of evaluating academic progress become necessary conditions for success. They also serve as important vehicles for encouraging faculty and administrators to break free from the way things have always been done, opening the door for rethinking the basic concept of seat time, or the long-standing practice of awarding academic credit for completing individual courses, or even the role of the individual faculty member and student in the learning process.

No wonder proposing and successfully implementing an integrated, competency-based three-year curriculum can be a demanding task, raising concerns, and in some cases evoking outright resistance from faculty members and administrators steeped in traditional approaches to curriculum design. So why should institutions pursue this option? One reason is that the process of fundamentally redesigning the traditional four-year undergraduate academic experience can be rewarding, inspiring, renewing, and enormously thought-provoking. Faculty members and academic leaders get to reconsider long-held views about how best to design and deliver their programs.

On a more practical level, unless the financial challenges families face to meet the expense of a college degree can be successfully overcome, the risk is that access to higher education will become limited to only those who can afford it without incurring large amounts of debt. However, if by addressing the financial challenges facing students and their families the quality of the educational experience is adversely affected, those graduating will not be as prepared as they need to be to succeed in their chosen careers or perhaps to pursue graduate study. The experience at Southern New Hampshire University has demonstrated that the Integrated, Competency-Based Degree Model can successfully address the financial concerns without sacrificing academic quality. The data collected over a ten-year period (which is presented in Chapter 5) clearly supports this statement. The remainder of this chapter will discuss the challenges of successfully designing and implementing this type of three-year-degree program.

As with any major change initiative, leaders at higher educational institutions seeking to offer this option need to anticipate criticisms, most likely significant and severe, from individuals both internal and external to the organization. The degree to which institutional leaders are willing and able to confront legitimate concerns from stakeholders and overcome any resistance will determine in large part whether an integrated, competency-based three-year program can be successful. It is crucial that these efforts begin at the design and implementation stages and continue until the new model is fully integrated into the institution. In order to accomplish this, a comprehensive change initiative needs to be launched concurrent with the curriculum redesign efforts. Fortunately, a number of change models can assist in these efforts. There is Kotter's eight-step change process (1996); Lewin's classic unfreezing, changing, refreezing approach (Schein, 2010); and Beckhard's (1969) model where dissatisfaction with the current state when multiplied by vision and first steps can overcome resistance.

Kotter's eight-step model was used to guide the design and implementation process at Southern New Hampshire University. The process starts with creating a sense of urgency about the need for change, followed by establishing a powerful coalition of key people to lead the change effort. These individuals need to represent a broad spectrum of the organization and be recognized and respected within it for their expertise, influence, and abilities. Once established, this team then helps to create a compelling, easily understood vision for the change and works tirelessly to communicate it to the various constituencies within the organization. Once a sense of urgency has been established, the team formed, and the vision created and communicated, the next important step is for institutional leaders to remove any obstacles that might block or impede change from occurring. The final three steps in Kotter's process are creating short-term wins, building upon early successes, and locking the change into the organization's culture.

Creating the Urgency

If "it ain't broke, don't fix it" is an often-heard expression in organizations, particularly those comfortable with the status quo. When things are going well, people are often reluctant to consider, let alone support, change. It is difficult to get people to change the way they have always done things when there is no immediate crisis demanding it. After all, nothing is broken that requires fixing. However, this is not the case in higher education today. Although there may be institutions that are not overly concerned about the potential for declining enrollments caused by the sticker shock of four years' worth of tuition expenses, there are many more that are greatly concerned. So it should come as no surprise that many of the recent conversations about three-year undergraduate-degree programs have, more often than not, been in response to concerns about the ever-rising tuition for a college degree. Will students be able to continue to afford a traditional four-year education? If not, how will institutions cope with the loss of enrollments? For many institutions, the three-year option is one way to ease the financial concerns of students and their families, while maintaining or perhaps even growing the institution's enrollment base.

In Chapters 5 and 7 the financial implications and cost structure of the different three-year models are discussed. The conclusion is that the Integrated Model can offer significant savings to students and their families while also reducing delivery costs for institutions. Kotter's sense of urgency can be legitimately created using the financial argument, particularly at tuition-driven institutions. Still, as important as revenue concerns may be in garnering support for change of this magnitude, this book argues that the integrated, competency-based three-year approach to undergraduate education should be much more than just a remedy for financial concerns.

For years one of the major criticisms leveled against college graduates is that they do not possess sufficient knowledge and skills to succeed in their careers. Concerns about written and oral communication skills, critical thinking, and the ability to work collaboratively are often given as examples of where many newly hired graduates fall short. The Association of American Colleges and Universities published a report, *Greater Expectations: A New Vision for Learning as a Nation Goes to College*, which noted that the changing nature of the workplace was putting pressure on higher educational institutions to ensure that graduates possess these skills and that, "inconsistent results lead employers to question higher education's effectiveness and wish that its degrees, like technical certification, ensured documented levels of accomplishment" (AAC&U, 2002, p. 8). The essence of the Integrated Model is that it is competency based and is designed to address these kinds of workforce readiness gaps. In a competency-based model, graduates need to demonstrate that they possess the program's competencies in order to earn their degrees. Creating a sense of urgency and getting buy-in from key stakeholders about how best to prepare young people to succeed in the twenty-first-century workforce may prove more appealing to educators as a call to action than the financial concerns, thus perhaps making it easier to create an integrated competency-based program.

The Integrated, Competency-Based Three-Year Model at Southern New Hampshire University (SNHU) was originally developed in 1996 with a U.S. Department of Education grant from the Fund for the Improvement of Postsecondary Education (FIPSE). Although the Department of Education was concerned about cost containment in higher education, it was equally concerned about the quality of the academic experience. The challenge presented to the grant applicants was to address the rising costs of a college education without compromising quality. The goal at SNHU was to reduce tuition by approximately 25 percent and institutional delivery costs by a similar amount by redesigning a traditional four-year bachelor of science degree in business administration into a competency-based three-year degree without adversely affecting the academic quality of the experience.

Initially, the students recruited to enroll in the program represented a new revenue stream for the institution, providing a strong financial incentive to proceed. The grant provided funding for faculty release time to take on the curriculum redesign responsibilities. The potential for new revenue, along with funding to assist in the redesign effort, were important first steps in gaining internal support. However, beyond the financial benefit for the institution and the anticipated savings to students and their families, it was the work the faculty did to address the concerns about how well college graduates are prepared for entry into the workforce that became the focal point.

To address these concerns, an extensive review of the literature was conducted to identify the key competencies that graduating students needed to possess upon completion of their degree programs. Guidelines from professional associations and professional and regional accreditation bodies were reviewed. Additionally, surveys were conducted to identify what employers believed were the most important competencies that graduates should possess. Finally, SNHU alumni were surveyed and asked to identify the competencies they had found to be most critical for success when they entered the workforce. All the results were reviewed by the design team and the dean's office, and ultimately a set of competencies that students would be expected to possess at graduation was identified and agreed upon.

The recognition that an undergraduate-degree program that could be completed in three years, saving students and their families a fourth year of tuition, and that was based on a set of competencies that would make its graduates more attractive candidates for employment convinced the university faculty that the hard work of redesigning the curriculum was a worthwhile endeavor and could make a real difference for the institution, its students, and its faculty. This unique value proposition was the key factor in garnering broad institution-wide support for moving forward.

Building Coalitions

Gaining support for moving a process forward is different from convincing people that it is necessary, or even desirable. To get people to embrace change requires strong, effective, and consistent leadership and, until the proposed change is fully embraced, the chances of success are very limited. With any change, some levels of resistance should be expected, ranging from relatively passive to more aggressive. However, when the proposed change is as significant as a three-year undergraduate-degree model, resistance needs to be identified early and overcome quickly in order to gain the broad institutional support needed for success. The key to overcoming resistance and gaining support is having the right team of people leading the effort. This group must include members from all the constituencies affected by the new model, and they need to be involved from the very outset. Beyond just representing all the interested parties, the members of this team need to be recognized by their colleagues as possessing the skills required for the task. As Kotter (1996) notes, team members leading the effort need to have the respect of their colleagues, the ability to influence others, and the authority to make decisions. To ensure that members have these qualities, they may need to be actively recruited to participate. The institution may also need to provide team members release time from teaching and administrative responsibilities and/or some additional compensation for their work.

At SNHU, the program chosen for the redesign effort was business administration, the largest undergraduate major at the institution. The rationale was that if a pilot three-year program in this discipline could be successfully launched, it would demonstrate that the model was achievable and would also become the template for other majors. One of the important principles for the redesign was that all general education and liberal arts requirements would remain critical components of the new program. There was no interest in eliminating, reducing, or deemphasizing any of these content areas. It was essential, therefore, that faculty members from both business and the arts and sciences disciplines be represented on the design team and be responsible for directing the curriculum redesign.

This cross-disciplinary group of faculty, along with key members of the administration, served as the design team, with one of the faculty appointed project director. Initially, the team was to consider the question, "Knowing what you know about higher education, undergraduate curricula, college students and faculty, and the desired outcomes of a college education, if you could do anything you wanted to improve the educational experience at this institution, what would it be?" Team members were encouraged not to be bound by existing practices and policies but to think differently about how to deliver quality academic programs. The fact that SNHU was only one of two schools in the nation, and the only private institution, to be awarded the FIPSE grant helped create a sense that what was being undertaken was unique and important and that breaking the mold was expected. Framing the discussion in this way helped to free the members of the team to think more creatively about how to approach the redesign of the curriculum. It also provided the foundation for what would become the vision statement used to gain broad support from the larger academic community and to begin to generate the momentum necessary for successful implementation.

Creating and Communicating the Vision

For any change to be successful, especially one with the potential to significantly impact an organization, it is essential that the people most affected by the change understand what their world will look like when it becomes reality. They need to understand what will be expected of them now and in the future and how the change will affect their lives. The more significant the change, the more critical it is to have these understandings in order to gain broad-based support within the organization. This future state and these expectations need to be communicated with simple, clear language and clarity of purpose. A vision statement is the way to do this. Beyond describing what will be, a vision statement helps those involved appreciate what they will be asked to do to achieve it.

Vision Statement

To deliver a student-centered, competency-based, undergraduate-degree program in six consecutive semesters that is nationally recognized for its innovation and excellence.

In communicating the vision, repetition is crucial. Those leading the change effort need to take every opportunity to reinforce the vision. People within the organization need to be reminded not only that the change is occurring but that they will play an important role in determining how successful it is. Additionally, acknowledging the many challenges inherent in a major change effort and addressing concerns and anxieties of those most affected is essential at this stage of the process. However, as critical as this reinforcement is, people also need to be kept apprised of what has been accomplished to date and what remains to be done to maintain and expand organizational support.

At SNHU, the members of the design team played a key role in articulating and reinforcing the vision of the three-year program to the internal community. Recognizing that most people are focused on their day-to-day responsibilities and filter out messages they do not see as critical to their jobs, the team developed elevator statements to describe in a few moments what the three-year concept was and the benefits it would bring to the university and its faculty and students. Using these statements, team members made it a point to talk about the three-year concept at every opportunity. Additionally, they made formal and informal presentations to numerous campus groups, including the university board of trustees, the undergraduate school's academic policy and curriculum committees, faculty and department meetings, and the admissions staff. All major committee meetings included updates on the status of the three-year initiative. Informal hallway and lunch-table conversations were commonplace.

Elevator Statement

The three-year model is an integrated, competency-based, 120-credit-hour undergraduate-degree program that can be completed in six consecutive semesters with no night, weekend, or summer coursework required. Students and their families save the tuition and expenses associated with a fourth year of study, while the institution also realizes significant savings in its program delivery costs. Additionally, a program built on competencies that better prepare graduates for success in their careers gives an added competitive advantage.

The meeting dates, times, and locations of the design team committee were posted in advance, and all meetings were open to all members of the faculty and administration. The agenda always included time for questions and comments from those in attendance. Formal minutes of all meetings were widely distributed. Team members also made themselves available to offer updates and answer questions at regularly scheduled open forums. One tool that proved particularly useful in the communication process was a detailed flowchart that mapped the developmental activities required to successfully implement the program (Appendix F). It helped both supporters and skeptics to better appreciate the magnitude of the undertaking while demonstrating how all the developmental elements fit together.

Removing Roadblocks, Showing Progress, and Building Momentum

Obstacles inhibiting or preventing change certainly can include resistance from people within the organization. But they also include institutional barriers that are often created by long-standing operational practices, which can make accomplishing change more difficult than it needs to be. As discussed previously in this chapter, overcoming resistance arising from individual concerns starts with having the right people leading the change effort, individuals respected by and able to influence their colleagues. However, when people are being asked to act in fundamentally different ways, it is also important to recognize that resistance can emanate from concerns about their ability to do what is being asked of them.

For example, the integrated three-year-degree program is built on competencies, utilizes learning communities, and requires a high level of collaboration among members of the teaching faculty. Some of these individuals may not be sufficiently knowledgeable about these concepts or appreciate how they will affect their teaching. In order to overcome resistance in cases such as these, more than respected and influential leaders are needed. Institutions must provide in-house professional development workshops, as well as external opportunities so that faculty can learn how to effectively incorporate new strategies and concepts into their teaching.

At SNHU, the initial professional development workshops focused on the Barr and Tagg (1995) concept of student-centered learning, where the student is at the center of the learning environment and the faculty members serve as facilitators of learning. The workshops were designed to provide a more in-depth understanding of these key concepts as well as to give those attending the opportunity to collaborate in identifying strategies that could be employed to create a student-centered learning environment. Additionally, numerous workshops were offered on writing academic plans. In particular, emphasis was placed on developing specific implementing activities that faculty could use in their classrooms to lay the foundation, serve as reinforcement, or assist with implementing one or more of the ten competencies intended as outcomes for their content area. (A more detailed description of what an academic plan entails is provided in Chapter 3.) External professional development opportunities occurred primarily during the program implementation stage. They most often involved faculty attending conferences on outcomes assessment and learning how they might better integrate assessment practices into their content areas. This was at a time when comprehensive outcomes assessment was a relatively new concept at most institutions.

Overcoming institutional barriers to change starts with a recognition that most organizations are bureaucratic in nature. The policies, procedures, and rules that are in place are intended to help ensure that the desired organizational outcomes are achieved. However, rigid adherence can sometimes restrict an organization's flexibility to respond to changing circumstances or try new approaches. One important task of a project leader is to identify when the normal way of doing business is hindering or preventing change and take corrective action.

At SNHU one of the design teams' first challenges was getting support for three-year students spending the first six weeks of their fall semester taking only two academic content areas: information technology and English composition. Traditionally, new full-time undergraduate students enrolled in five courses at the start of their fall semester, and two of these typically were introductory courses in information technology and English composition. The faculty experts believed that if students were totally immersed in information technology and English composition in their first weeks, they would build a stronger foundation and be better prepared for their other course work. No one expressed concerns about the efficacy of this approach. Indeed, there was much support. However, three-year students would earn six credits by mid-October and then begin new courses. The concerns raised were about room scheduling, full-time billing, registration, and financial aid—in other words, policies, rules, and procedures. The project leader worked with the appropriate administrative offices to address the concerns and did not allow them to prevent the three-year idea from being implemented.

Although the reason for awarding credit early in the fall semester was academic considerations, one interesting consequence of doing so has been an increase in student satisfaction and retention. As Pritchard, Wilson, and Yamnitz (2007) note it is common for some first-semester college students to withdraw within the first six weeks of the fall semester. No three-year students at SNHU have done so. Instead, these students report that earning credits earlier than any of their four-year counterparts is highly motivating.

In some cases, the senior leadership of an organization must step in and remove the obstacles impeding progress. Redesigning an existing curriculum model and moving it successfully through the academic governance processes at most higher educational institutions can be a daunting task. Typically, the process takes an entire academic year or more, once the program is actually developed and submitted for approval. It is certainly reasonable for those evaluating a proposal to expect that academic quality will not be adversely affected by the new approach. They want assurances that students will perform as well or better than before and that any expected benefits will be realized. How does one provide data that demonstrates quality, performance, and benefits before actually implementing the program?

At SNHU, the president elected to treat the proposed three-year program as a pilot program. The undergraduate curriculum committee would receive and review all related three-year documents, be able to raise any questions or concerns with members of the design team, and engage in three-year discussions. But it was decided that the committee would not be asked to formally approve the program until after the first entering class had graduated and the data was available to evaluate. This proved to be one of the more significant decisions. It allowed the program to move forward and provided it with crucial time and space to demonstrate its value. It is important to note that the decision to put off formal approval until after implementation would likely not be possible at all institutions. An organizational climate where relationships among the president, academic administration, and faculty were positive made it possible. One result of this decision was an increased awareness of the importance of building support by providing as much information as possible.

A faculty steering committee was established to oversee the implementation of the program. One of the first decisions of the steering committee was to commit to full transparency. So, as was the case with the design team, minutes of steering committee meetings were made available through multiple venues. A three-year newsletter was created and became the primary vehicle for communicating all relevant three-year information to the broader community and making the case for the program's success. As data became available—for example, retention statistics for first semester to second semester and for first year to second year—they were disseminated via the newsletter. Entering-class profiles, including average SAT scores, GPAs, high school class ranks, and geographic data, were also published.

The steering committee determined that one of the best ways to achieve transparency and to document and build upon success was to open the end-of-the-semester integrating experience presentations to the entire community, as well as to invited external guests. The presentations were also recorded. Anyone present or viewing the presentations could judge the quality for themselves. The decision to open the presentations to the public proved extremely valuable because those attending became some of the most enthusiastic advocates for the three-year program and helped generate additional internal and external support for continuing it.

Sometimes, the most challenging obstacles are not as obvious as individual resistance, inflexible administrative practices, or slow-moving governance processes. They are the obstacles that come from misleading or inaccurate information that becomes part of the discussions. For example, two statements that continued to resurface in the first years of the program at SNHU were "The program is very expensive and loses money" and "Faculty, administrative, and other limited resources are being taken away from other programs to support this one." They were made as statements of fact, which if left unchallenged would have been poisonous, and support for the program continuing and growing would have eroded. In keeping with their commitment to open communication, the steering committee made all financial information related to the three-year program available for review. In addition, an external consultant was hired to conduct a complete financial audit, and data and analyses were widely disseminated through both formal and informal channels. The results put to rest any concerns about the financial viability of the program. It did not lose money, even when an intentionally higher overhead charge was assessed. It generated a profit. The audit also helped to dispel the notion that resources were being diverted from other programs.

Institutionalizing the Change

In some sense, the urgency called for at the outset of a change initiative is just as important at this last stage, perhaps even more so. Until any new initiative becomes a core part of the organization, it remains at risk. People are creatures of habit and tend to revert to their comfort zones, particularly when under pressure. For change to become institutionalized, it often requires that organizational systems be redesigned in order that the desired new behaviors and methods can be rewarded and reinforced. The biggest mistake organizations can make is to declare victory too early.

At SNHU, gaining full acceptance of the three-year program from the university community was made easier by the results that are described in Chapter 5. Students did save 25 percent in tuition charges and, as measured by the Educational Testing Service (ETS) Major Field Tests, the average scores of these students were not significantly different from the national scores. The institution did reduce its program delivery costs, and the retention and graduation rates of three-year students consistently exceeded the national averages. However, the sign that the three-year program was becoming deeply woven into the fabric of the institution was when initiatives, practices, and ideas that were initially seen as "three-year only" began to be adopted school- and university-wide.

The first example of three-year ideas becoming mainstream was in 2001 when the business faculty engaged in a school-wide strategic planning process and voted to adopt the ten competencies as the foundation for all business majors. As a result of this decision, department faculty needed to ensure that the competencies were being addressed in all business programs, and they were asked to document how and to what extent they were being addressed. This led to the use of the process for identifying course-level learning outcomes described in Chapter 2 and, ultimately, to the adoption of the academic planning documents that were central to the development of the three-year curriculum. Today, all new course proposals in the business school require that an academic plan and a model syllabus be included as part of the formal curriculum approval process. So in essence, three fundamental concepts of the Integrated Three-Year Program, described in greater detail in the next chapter—integration, competencies, and academic planning documents—are now part of normal operating practices at the institution.

A smaller example, certainly by contemporary standards, of the three-year program becoming part of the mainstream of university life was the adoption of a laptop computer requirement. A debate had been raging among the business faculty for a number of years about requiring all business students to come to the university with laptop computers, but there was never consensus. By design, the three-year curriculum was technology intensive. From the first entering class, three-year students were required to have laptop computers, and where appropriate, all of their modules along with the integrating experiences and senior project incorporated the use of laptops and other technology. Although there were some initial challenges related to classroom management and technical support, neither the faculty nor the students reported any major issues over the years. So in 2005, after eight years of three-year laptop use, when a new business school dean asked the faculty to support a policy of requiring all business students to come to campus with laptops, consensus was quickly reached and the requirement adopted. Two years later the university adopted the laptop requirement for all of its entering undergraduate students.

Change is a never-ending process. Almost a decade and a half after the launch of the SNHU Integrated, Competency-Based Three-Year Program and the kinds of success described in Chapter 5, the work to ensure that it remains a core part of the institution goes on. As new faculty and administrators join the university and some of the early supporters of the three-year program depart, communicating the vision to ensure that understanding and support is maintained is as important today as it was when the program was first conceived; so too is identifying and removing any new obstacles that might appear. And as the data demonstrating the program's success continues to be shared with both internal and external stakeholders, the three-year model will be firmly established in the ethos of the institution.

5

Results, Analysis, and Proof of Concept

Measuring outcomes and assessing effectiveness are important components of any serious program evaluation effort. In the case of three-year-degree programs, the evaluation effort needs to demonstrate to both internal and external stakeholders that the promised financial advantages do indeed exist and that degree requirements can be completed within three years. Beyond these two factors, institutions offering three-year programs also need to address the question of academic performance. For example, do three-year students perform at least as well in their programs of study as their four-year counterparts, and how is this determined?

Questions about workforce readiness and job placement also need to be addressed. How prepared are these students to enter today's job market? How successful are they at finding jobs once they graduate? Other relevant questions concern life outside of the classroom. Do students accelerating their degree completion have time to join and participate in student organizations? Are they able to hold student leadership positions? Do they participate in intercollegiate athletics or serve as volunteers or mentors? All these questions are important. And when the program being evaluated not only speeds up the time for degree completion but also fundamentally changes the design and delivery of the traditional four-year undergraduate university experience, as is the case with integrated programs, a comprehensive evaluation effort is essential to demonstrate that the benefits to both students and the institution are clear and compelling.

This chapter examines the financial implications of three-year-degree programs from the perspective of the students and their families, as well as the institution. Also discussed is how to evaluate the effectiveness of these programs using student academic performance, retention and graduation rates, workforce and graduate school readiness, and participation in student life as key measures. Finally, data on the outcomes experienced at Southern New Hampshire University's Integrated Three-Year-Degree Program are presented and discussed.

Financial Considerations for Students and Families

Although the academic performance of the students should ultimately determine the success of any three-year delivery model, the reason most often cited for accelerating completion of one's degree is to mitigate the continually escalating cost of a college education. The idea of saving a fourth year of tuition and fees and entering the workforce one year sooner is very attractive to many students. Yet does completing a three-year-degree program really translate into any significant tuition savings to students and their families?

In the Accelerated Model presented in Chapter 1, the path to degree attainment is definitely faster, giving students earlier entry into the job market and their careers. But in order to earn all the required credits in three years, students typically must take extra courses during a semester, at night, online, on weekends, and/or during the summer. They may be charged some additional tuition for these courses, so the savings in overall tuition may be relatively minor. The real savings in this type of model is for students who live in campus housing. By completing degree requirements in three years, resident students eliminate the fourth year of room and board charges and associated fees.

The Prior Learning approach, also presented in Chapter 1, leads to faster degree completion. In this model, students receive credit by demonstrating that they have acquired knowledge equivalent to college-level courses. This is most often achieved by taking CLEP or Advanced Placement examinations or by taking the equivalent of college-level courses through a dual-enrollment partnership between their high school and a higher educational institution. Some prior-learning models also award credit for work experience. By awarding prior-learning credit for ten courses, which is roughly the equivalent of one academic year, students save one year's tuition. However, there are costs associated with taking CLEP and Advanced Placement examinations, and some institutions charge an assessment fee to evaluate the documentation to support the awarding of prior-learning credits for work experience. Students receiving credit for fewer than ten courses find it necessary to accelerate their studies in order to complete degree requirements in three years. As is the case with the Accelerated Model, on-campus resident students in the Prior Learning Model can reduce their overall expenses by eliminating the fourth year of room, board, and fee charges.

In the Integrated Model, degree requirements are also satisfied over a six-semester period or its equivalent. And as with the previous two models, the degree path is faster, and resident students do not incur the room and board expenses of a fourth year. The key difference is in the design of the Integrated Model, which allows students to earn credits through competency demonstration and not by just taking individual courses during the semester. As a result, students are not required to take courses at nights, on weekends, or in the summers, nor are they assessed any additional tuition charges during their three years. The result is a 25 percent tuition savings to students and their families plus any savings associated with living on campus. This is much more than what is typically experienced in Accelerated or Prior Learning Models, where there may be additional charges for the extra courses or prior-learning certification, respectively.

Financial Considerations for Institutions

When considering the adoption of a three-year-degree option, college and university leaders need to carefully evaluate the pros and cons of each model. Given the particular circumstances at their institutions and the conditions in the external environment, they need to determine which one is most appropriate. As more colleges and universities add a three-year option to their menu of program offerings, the financial impact could end up making or breaking the institution.

Accelerated Three-Year-Degree Considerations

What about the financial implications from an institutional perspective? Can an Accelerated Three-Year-Degree Model be financially viable? Yes. If the institution charges four years of tuition for three years of attendance, as is the case with some accelerated programs, then the institution loses no tuition revenue. However, there could be a loss of auxiliary service revenue, such as room and board fees that would have been generated by students residing in on-campus housing for the fourth year unless the beds are filled by other students. Four years' worth of tuition would possibly cover the added costs to the institution of providing additional sections that may be needed to guarantee students are able to graduate in three years. Note that three-year students, who will essentially be paying a 33 percent annual tuition premium, are sitting in the same classes as their four-year classmates who will not be paying the additional amount. Whether this disparity will help or hinder three-year student recruitment remains to be seen. All things being equal, given the choice of paying four years' worth of tuition in one university's three-year program versus paying only three years' worth of tuition in another school's three-year program, the 25 percent tuition savings will likely influence school decisions.

If the fourth year of tuition is eliminated or significantly reduced, then the financial impact on the institution could be significant unless the students in the three-year program represent a new revenue stream—meaning that they would not otherwise have chosen to enroll at the institution. Three years' worth of tuition may not offset any added course delivery costs to the institution. To offset this loss of tuition revenue, institutions would need a similar reduction in their delivery costs. On the other hand, a 25 percent tuition savings might be attractive and help with admissions.

Prior Learning Three-Year-Degree Considerations

This model is a special case of the Accelerated Model when it comes to financial considerations. Assuming that students arrive with the equivalent of thirty credits, they can be considered to be like sophomore transfers, and the institution might not have to add additional courses and time slots for this group. However, the lower the number of equivalent prior-learning credits upon entry, the more additional course delivery costs may be incurred by the institution to ensure that the students graduate on time. It is assumed that prior-learning students would not pay a four-year tuition premium and that their annual tuition would be the same as their four-year peers.

Integrated Three-Year-Degree Considerations

The institution will need to consider the up-front costs of curriculum redesign necessary to implement a three-year program or programs. These costs may include faculty release time, dedicated professional development funds, administrative coordination costs, and additional expenses for marketing and recruitment. But after that, the savings in course delivery costs makes the Integrated Three-Year-Degree Model a winner for the institution. Here's how.

Suppose that the four years' worth of tuition is charged for the three-year-degree students. Then they will pay an annual 33 percent tuition premium, but as this book shows, the institution will have reduced its course delivery costs by as much as 25 percent. This is a big win for the institution: more annual revenue, lower annual costs. On the other hand, suppose that the three-year-degree students pay exactly the same tuition each year as the four-year-degree students pay and complete all of their degree requirements in three years. Then, because of the annual course delivery cost reductions, the institution still comes out ahead. These cost savings due to the Integrated Model might also mitigate the potential loss of auxiliary services revenue such as the room and board fees that would have been generated by students residing in on-campus housing for the fourth year, unless as noted previously, the beds are filled by other students.

The Integrated Three-Year Model can be financially beneficial for both students and institutions. With this model, whether three or four years of tuition are charged, students and their families can be assured that the integrated, competency-based education provides a comprehensive educational experience that prepares students for successful professional careers and beyond.

Beyond Financial Considerations

A number of other issues beyond the financial ones must also be addressed to evaluate the efficacy of three-year delivery models. Earning an undergraduate degree in three years as opposed to four is clearly faster, and graduates of these programs can and do enter the workforce one year earlier or have the opportunity to earn their graduate degrees sooner. Direct entry into the workforce gives these students one year of earnings advantage over their contemporaries as well as a head start on loan repayments. Yet even with the financial savings and the opportunity to enter the workforce or a graduate program a year earlier, important questions remain.

Is the educational experience in a three-year program at least as good as that in a traditional four-year program? Is the academic performance of students in three-year programs negatively affected by speeding up their graduation date? Are graduates from these programs as prepared as their four-year counterparts for entry into the job market or graduate school? And are these students able to participate in extracurricular and co-curricular activities and fully experience college life? Institutions offering the three-year-degree options will need to provide answers to these questions in order to address the concerns of their various constituencies. The following sections discuss academic performance, retention and graduation rates, workforce readiness, and student life as potential measures for evaluating the effectiveness of three-year programs.

Academic Performance and Success of Students

Regardless of the type of three-year program—Accelerated, Prior Learning, or Integrated—the academic performance and ultimate success of the students are the most critical factors in determining its worth. In assessing academic performance, it is important for institutions to answer the questions raised above concerning any negative effects that might result from speeding up one's degree completion and how three-year students compare to four-year students in terms of academic performance. How best is this accomplished? These assessments should be conducted at both the program and individual level, using both direct and indirect measures. Direct measures might include standardized national tests and student portfolios, and indirect ones could be student, employer, and alumni surveys (Walvoord, 2010).

The Educational Testing Service (ETS) Major Field Tests is an example of a direct assessment measure using a standardized national test. Many colleges and universities use ETS to measure student academic achievement and growth as well as to assess the educational outcomes of programs. According to Banta (2007a), the benefits of standardized tests include greater availability, reliability, and validity than most instructor-developed tests as well as the normative data provided for student comparisons. There is a cost associated with most of these types of tests, and as Banta (2007a) also notes, because these tests need to be "administered in a time-constrained environment, they cannot cover all the aspects of college students' learning in a given major. Thus, they must be supplemented by other measures designed or selected by departmental faculty" (p. 6).

Retention and graduation rates are two important measures most often used to determine student success and institutional effectiveness. These rates have recently attracted attention at the national level. Berger and Lyon (2005) note that accreditation agencies require institutions to report their retention statistics, and Basken and Field (2008) report in a *Chronicle of Higher Education* article that student loans are now being tied to, among other factors, an institution's graduation rate. Given this attention, one can expect increasing emphasis on these two indicators of success.

Retention can be measured on a year-to-year basis by looking at the number of students who remain at the same institution from beginning to end. It can also be measured system-wide, that is, the number of students remaining enrolled at some higher educational institution from year to year but not at the same institution. There is also retention within majors and even retention within courses (Hagedorn, 2005).

The ultimate measure of academic success for students and effectiveness for institutions is degree attainment or graduation. So if students are successfully completing all program requirements and being awarded degrees, then by the graduation measure, they have succeeded. But for three-year students, another question needs to be answered. Are they truly graduating with their degrees in three years?

Institutional graduation rates reflect the percentage of students who earn their degrees from the institution where they began their studies. The 1990 Student Right-to-Know and Campus Security

Act requires higher educational institutions to report their graduation rates. At four-year-degree-granting institutions, this rate is measured over a six-year period, that is, the percentage of students who begin as freshmen and graduate with a baccalaureate degree within six years from the date of initial enrollment.

It is important for institutions that offer a three-year-degree option, whether the Accelerated, Prior Learning, or Integrated Model, to report both retention and graduation rates for these programs so that students, their families, and the general public can make informed choices.

Workforce and Graduate School Readiness

Clearly, one of the purposes of a college education is to prepare graduates for entry into their professional lives. And certainly, most students and their families expect that their college education will do so. For most students and their families, and particularly those who are taking on significant debt to finance their education, getting a job after graduation or gaining admission to graduate school is of paramount concern. A three-year-degree program may lessen the financial burdens, but beyond reducing costs, these programs—whether Accelerated, Prior Learning, or Integrated—must prepare students to enter and succeed in today's workforce. It is common for colleges and universities to report the percentage of their graduates who gain employment after earning their degrees or who are accepted into graduate programs. Many also report this data by schools or majors. As the number of three-year programs grows, institutions offering them will also be expected to provide this information. However, to address the concern that "less can't be as good," additional measures of success will likely be needed to demonstrate workforce and graduate school readiness.

Portfolios are another method institutions can use to measure the workforce and graduate school readiness of their graduates. Portfolios are a collection of work samples gathered over time that assist

in documenting student progress, accomplishments, and achievement in one or more areas of the curriculum. Many are electronic
and are provided to potential employers and graduate schools during the job search or admissions process as a means of demonstrating
the knowledge, skills, and abilities of the applicant.

Competency assessment is another means of documenting a
student's readiness to enter the workforce or begin graduate studies. Competencies are first identified and then the outcomes that
demonstrate the attainment of each competency are described,
along with the methods used for assessment. Multiple methods are
available for institutions to use in assessing student performance
and competency attainment. Volkwein (2010), in his book on assessing student outcomes, provides information on the advantages
of a number of these methods, including capstone courses, senior
projects, portfolios, student self-evaluations, comprehensive exams,
and alumni studies. Administrators and faculty need to identify
which assessment methods are best for their institutions and then
begin to use them. Over time, the data will be valuable in assessing
student performance and in establishing benchmarks for comparing performance to previous years. Assessment efforts can also be
useful in identifying areas of concern and in focusing efforts on how
to improve.

Student Life

One of the early concerns expressed by students, families, and institutions about completing an undergraduate degree in three years
was whether students pursuing a three-year curriculum would have
the time and opportunity to fully participate in college life, thus
developing and maturing as a result of both their academic and
non-academic experiences. As noted earlier, with most accelerated
models, students need to take additional courses each semester or at
night, on weekends, or during summers in order to complete degree
requirements within three years. This acceleration may make it
difficult for some students to hold much-needed jobs to meet their

higher education financial obligations as well as enjoy a robust life outside of the classroom.

With prior-learning models, where students may be awarded thirty credits, or the equivalent of a full year, as they enter their first year, they would be like a second-year student taking a normal course load for the remaining six semesters. In these cases, there should be no barriers to full participation in student life. However, if students are awarded fewer prior learning credits than thirty, they will have less time to participate in a full range of extracurricular and co-curricular activities.

Integrated models like the one at SNHU do not require students to take courses at night, on weekends, or during summers in order to complete their degree requirements in three years. However, these models do require students to earn additional credits in each of their six semesters. These credits are earned in a variety of different ways but not by taking additional courses. Rather, credits are earned by demonstrating competency in specific academic content areas. As mentioned in Chapter 3, public speaking can be incorporated into multiple courses with students awarded credit upon completion of the requirements by providing their faculty with appropriate documentation for review and evaluation. For example, the documentation could be in the form of a portfolio that might include video files of presentations and documents of different types of speeches.

Even so, because of the need for students to acquire and demonstrate the competencies, the question about college life outside of the classroom remains. Institutions offering three-year programs regardless of type need to provide information on the experiences of their students so that the students and their families fully appreciate what they may be sacrificing in order to earn their degrees in three years. In the case of the integrated three-year degree at SNHU discussed in the remainder of this chapter, the program design features provide students with many opportunities to participate in a wide variety of activities outside of the classroom.

Three-Year Program Results at SNHU

When the three-year-degree program was developed at SNHU, a number of outcomes were identified as indicators of effectiveness. These included savings to students and their families by reducing total tuition from four years to three years, a savings of 25 percent; savings to the institution by a similar reduction in program delivery costs; retention and graduation rates at or near the national norms; and academic performance of participants in the program at least equal to four-year students as measured by the Educational Testing Service Major Business Field Tests. In addition, other important outcomes included the validation of the three-year program by the university's accreditation bodies; workforce and graduate school readiness of graduates as determined by employers and admissions into graduate schools; the value of the program competencies as assessed annually by the alumni; and finally, the opportunity for three-year students to fully participate in extracurricular and co-curricular activities. The results are impressive and compelling, and in the following sections each of these desired outcomes is discussed in greater detail.

Financial Benefit to Students, Families, and Institutions

Although three-year students earn the same number of credits required of all four-year students earning baccalaureate degrees at SNHU, they incur no additional tuition charges or other fees for earning these credits in three years, as they would at some three-year programs. The integrated, competency-based curriculum design discussed in Chapter 3 makes this possible in several ways, including academic credit for demonstration of competency attainment as determined by the teaching faculty, through the end-of-semester integrating experiences and the applied management project during the entire third year of the program. As a result, room, board, tuition, and fee charges for a fourth year are eliminated, resulting in a 25 percent savings to students and their families. In addition to the savings of a fourth year of education, these students are able to enter the workforce one year earlier than their four-year counterparts, gaining both a salary and experience advantage. Those students who go directly on to graduate school can complete their studies one year earlier than their four-year counterparts.

The university also experiences savings as a result of reduced delivery costs. Two content areas, equivalent to six academic credits and delivered as discrete courses in the four-year program, are integrated throughout the year-one experience in the three-year program. A total of six academic credits is also awarded for the end-of-semester integrating experiences in years one and two. The faculty members teaching in each semester of the first two years of the program are responsible for designing, facilitating, and evaluating the integrating experiences as part of their regular teaching responsibilities. The third year includes a nine-credit senior experiential learning project in which students work as members of intact project teams under the supervision of a faculty facilitator. Students are matched with agencies, organizations, or business enterprises that have needs or projects relating to one or more academic content areas completed by the team members during their program. Finally, nine credits are earned when three-year students take elective courses with their four-year peers.

All these program features translate into a total of thirty credits being awarded to three-year program students without the institution incurring any significant additional delivery costs. Additionally, in the case of SNHU, over 80 percent of three-year students have reported that without the three-year option, they would not have enrolled at the institution. So essentially a new tuition revenue stream was created, just over $2 million in 2010–2011. When direct delivery costs and overhead charges are allocated, the three-year program, with its approximately 90 students, contributes significant tuition revenue to the institution's bottom line. Not included in this discussion is any revenue received for auxiliary services (such as room and board). Approximately, 75 percent of three-year students have historically lived in on-campus housing. Using the lowest 2010–2011 dormitory rates and a typical meal plan, this results in an additional $500,000 in auxiliary service revenue to the institution, because these students would not have been enrolled if there had been no three-year program.

Academic Performance and Success of Students

Students in the SNHU three-year-degree program in business administration take the ETS Major Field Tests in the fall of their third year. These exams are designed to measure student academic achievement and growth in the business disciplines. In addition, academic departments use them to evaluate the curriculum as part of their ongoing assessment efforts. Faculty also use them to measure their students' progress and provide students with an assessment of their level of achievement within their fields of study. These exams have been administered to all SNHU graduating students since 2001 as the primary direct measure of program and individual student success.

The content for these exams reflects the basic knowledge and understanding gained in the undergraduate business curriculum. They have been designed to assess the mastery of concepts, principles, and knowledge that students are expected to demonstrate at the conclusion of study in the major content area. For example, the business field test contains eight sub-areas of focus: accounting, economics, management, quantitative business analysis, finance, marketing, legal and social environment, and international issues (Educational Testing Service, 2011). In addition to assessing factual knowledge in the content areas, the major field test validates the students' ability to analyze and solve problems, understand relationships, and interpret material. The test may contain questions that require interpretation of graphs, diagrams, and charts based on material related to the field (Seidman & Bradley, 2002).

The average ETS test scores for SNHU three-year students in the second- and third-year cohorts were slightly above the national

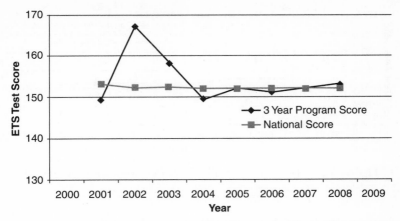

Figure 5.1. Comparison of ETS Test Performance (Score)

scores but have fluctuated near the national scores during the rest of the years, as Figure 5.1 shows.

Before testing, if there was a statistical difference in the average scores of SNHU three-year students and the national scores on the ETS test, the equal variance assumption for the two sets of scores was tested. The assumption was rejected very strongly at a p-value < 0.01. In other words, there was much greater variability in the average scores of the three-year students than in the national scores. Hence, a two-sample Welch t-test assuming unequal variances was conducted. The results showed no significant difference between the average scores of SNHU three-year students and the national scores on the ETS test. See Appendix 5: Comparison of Results of the ETS Major Field Test in Business Administration at http://www.josseybass.com/go/martinbradley.

Comparison of Three-Year Percentile Scores with National Percentile Scores on the ETS Test

The average percentile scores of SNHU three-year students on the ETS test were slightly above the national scores for the first three cohorts but have fluctuated near the national percentile scores since

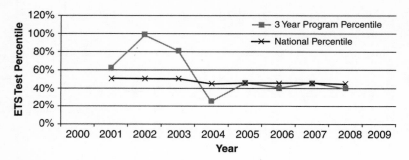

Figure 5.2. Comparison of ETS Test Performance (Percentile)

then, except in 2004. In that year, the average percentile score of SNHU three-year students experienced a dip down to the 25th percentile, as shown in Figure 5.2.

Before testing, if there was a statistical difference in the average percentile scores of SNHU three-year students and the national scores, the equal variance assumption for the two sets of scores was tested. The equal variance assumption was rejected very strongly at a p-value < 0.01. In other words, there was much greater variability in the average percentile scores for SNHU three-year students than in the national percentile scores. Hence, a two-sample Welch t-test assuming unequal variances was conducted. The results show no significant difference in the average percentile scores of SNHU three-year students and the national percentile scores on the ETS test.

Retention Rates

The SNHU three-year program, with its emphasis on students and faculty as members of a learning community, creates an environment that supports conditions for improved retention as described by Tinto (1999) and Seidman (2005). Unlike many retention programs that focus only on the first year, the SNHU three-year learning community is ongoing. Each new cohort of entering students becomes an individual community and joins the second- and third-year cohorts in the larger learning community of three-year students. In addition to their teaching responsibilities, faculty members act as mentors and facilitators of the learning process. They collaborate with their colleagues to create a greater synergy among the academic disciplines and establish overarching themes for each semester. These themes serve to give greater focus and better connect the material being taught. And together faculty constitute a learning community of their own, typically meeting weekly or biweekly to create integrative assignments and learning experiences, discuss student progress, and raise any issues of concern.

The results are impressive. First- to second-year retention rates for the SNHU three-year program consistently exceed the national averages. As described in Appendix B, the U.S. national retention rate in 2008 for four-year-degree students in private institutions offering only bachelor's and master's degrees with "traditional" selectivity was 70.5 percent (ACT, 2010b). In the same comparison year, the first- to second-year retention rate for students in the three-year program at Southern New Hampshire University was 80.6 percent (Bradley & Painchaud, 2009). The overall first- to second-year retention rate for the history of the program to date is 86.45 percent.

Additionally, the number of students returning in the second year has kept pace with the number of entering students. As the number of entering students has increased gradually over the last ten years, the number of students retained in the program has also increased. The retention rate, measured as the ratio of the number returning in the second year to the number originally entering in the cohort, has experienced a small and gradual decline over the years but has remained above 80 percent.

Graduation Rates

At 78.5 percent, the three-year program graduation rate through 2010 is well above the four-year national average of 39.2 percent for private institutions offering only bachelor's and master's degrees with "traditional" selectivity, and higher than the five-year and six-year graduation rates of 50.4 percent and 52.1 percent, respectively (see Appendix B; ACT, 2010c). It is important to note that the 78.5 percent figure is for students earning degrees in three years after the initial date of enrollment. It is also interesting to note that over a third of those students who left the three-year program remained enrolled at the institution and nearly all have earned their degrees.

Alumni and Employer Data

When the program competencies were first developed, the design team sought input from business and industry leaders who had for years been expressing concerns about the preparedness of college graduates entering the workforce (Casner-Lotto, Rosenblum, & Wright, 2009). The team gathered numerous professional societies' curricular recommendations, studied related research, surveyed existing competency-based programs, and sought ideas from faculty colleagues. They analyzed and synthesized this information, resulting in the ten school-level competencies presented in Chapter 2 that students must acquire in order to attain an undergraduate degree in business administration.

As part of an annual assessment effort at the end of each academic year, SNHU alumni are asked to complete a survey that measures how their education has contributed to the development of their skill level for each of the ten program competencies. Employers of SNHU graduates are also surveyed annually to determine the importance they place on these same competencies and to evaluate the degree to which their SNHU employees meet their expectations in each of the competencies. The responses from both groups confirm the importance and value of an integrated, competency-based curriculum that includes teamwork, problem solving, strategy, leadership, and communication among the competencies. The results are widely shared within the university community and are used to modify course academic plans as appropriate.

External Accreditation Associations

Since its inception, the SNHU three-year program has been reviewed by the university's external accreditation organizations as part of the normal review process of the institution, the Business School, and the program offerings. These organizations include the New England Association of Secondary Schools and Colleges (NEASC) and two international business professional school accreditation bodies. The program has received very favorable comments, in particular for its innovative design, implementation, and approach to learning. The NEASC report (2001) noted:

> A new three year competency-based intensive BS degree program in business administration . . . is offered on campus and is the first of its kind in the country. Preliminary evaluations, using a national standardized test, indicate student outcomes equal or better than those of students in the traditional four-year business administration degree program. (pp. 10–11)

The report also described the program as one of the institution's undergraduate program strengths, observing, "The innovative three year accelerated Business Administration Program has clearly articulated competency-based outcomes and uses a series of integrating experiences at the end of each semester to assess these outcomes" (p. 11).

Extracurricular Involvement

Students enrolled in the Integrated Three-Year Program at SNHU report the need for effective time management skills in order to meet the program's academic requirements. However, over the nearly decade and a half of the program's history, three-year students have indeed been fully engaged members of the university community. They have been active in many of the campus student organizations, often serving in leadership positions. These include the student government association, fraternity and sorority life, NCAA Division II athletic programs, honor societies, and the student newspaper. They have served as resident assistants in the dormitories, as well as orientation leaders and student ambassadors. And they are always represented in volunteer efforts undertaken by the student body such as disaster relief fundraisers, cancer awareness walk-a-thons, and alternative spring breaks. So although they complete their undergraduate education in three years, they seem not to do so at the expense of opportunities to participate in and benefit from the full range of college experiences.

Recap

Competency assessment is important work and is best approached using multiple means of assessment. The direct and indirect assessment strategies discussed in this chapter have been employed to determine the strengths and weaknesses of the nation's first integrated, competency-based three-year curriculum. In addition to evaluating the effectiveness of this innovative curriculum model, the critical non-academic components that encompass the out-of-class student experience have also been examined. The conclusion is that since the inception of the program in 1997, most students have successfully completed their bachelor's degree on time while participating in the many important facets of student life outside the classroom.

After graduation, students have gone on to successfully begin their careers, or earn graduate degrees before starting their professional lives. Each year, alumni and employers report favorably on the three-year program competencies and the role that they play in their professions.

As the program continues to evolve, ongoing and improved assessment measures will add to the depth and breadth of the data collection and analysis process. These activities will give additional perspective on other positive aspects that an intentionally designed, integrated, competency-based three-year curriculum can provide for students ready to undertake their collegiate journey on this kind of academic path. Already the formative and summative assessment measures currently used have led to adjustments to the curriculum and program structure, thus ensuring continued student academic success and, just as important, student satisfaction with out-of-class university experiences.

6

Value-Added Dimensions of
Integrated Three-Year Degrees

W hereas Chapters 2 and 3 presented the necessary core components underlying the Integrated Three-Year Model, this
chapter discusses several interrelated value-added dimensions that,
from experience, can help ensure the success of that model.

By organizing students into cohorts that move together from
one module to another, a dynamic learning community with all
its attendant advantages can be created. Within student learning
communities, intact student work groups can be formed for cross-
disciplinary work inside and outside the physical classroom. Just as
students can form learning communities, so too can their teachers.
Professional learning communities encourage collaboration across
disciplines to the benefit of both students and faculty, and they afford faculty the opportunity to keep close tabs on students' progress
toward achieving the competencies within and across modules.
Semester and yearlong academic themes serve as a common ground-
ing for these learning communities and the learning experiences
associated with a variety of modules.

In addition, the learning paradigm promoted by Barr and Tagg's
seminal article "From Teaching to Learning: A New Paradigm for
Undergraduate Education" (1995) and Tagg's book *The Learning
Paradigm College* (2003) can serve the Integrated Three-Year Model
well because it entails active learning, is outcomes driven, and en-
courages student collaborative and cooperative work for maximum

learning effectiveness. A virtual collaborative environment's technological infrastructure can extend the classroom through time and space and can facilitate the learning paradigm as well as the other value-added dimensions discussed in this chapter. A virtual collaborative environment ensures that breaking the bonds of seat time in the Integrated Model does not necessarily entail less meaningful instructor-student and student-student contact and interaction. In addition, due to the nature of the learning paradigm, formative and summative outcomes assessments are keys to the success of the Integrated Model.

The chapter closes with walkthroughs of each of the three-year program's years from the perspectives of students and their teaching faculty. These walkthroughs give a flavor for how these dimensions add important value to the students' educational experiences and how learning outcomes can be achieved more effectively and efficiently.

Value-Added Dimensions

These value-added dimensions can help to ensure the success of an integrated three-year-degree program. They are time-tested dimensions, but they are particularly suited for an environment where seat time is no longer the standard for academic advancement and where competency-based learning is primary. They also can help to retain students. The retention literature shows that student groups and academic support systems through linked classes facilitate student retention. In addition, effective assessment of student progress toward educational outcomes and cooperative/collaborative teaching strategies plus learning communities also support retention (Tinto, 1998, 1999, 2006–2007; Seidman, 2005).

Student Cohorts and Learning Communities

Learning Communities: Reforming Undergraduate Education (Smith, MacGregor, Matthews, & Gabelnick, 2004) describes the extensive research literature on the benefits of student cohorts and learning communities. These benefits include enhanced student learning, improved curricular coherence, and the rejuvenation of participating faculty. Students who move together through various modules in a semester get to know one another and have more sustained opportunities to work together than if they were not in a cohort. Student cohorts provide teachers with the opportunity to work together in professional learning communities to create joint assignments that span modules and disciplines. In addition, teachers have opportunities to see the students from multiple academic perspectives. Faculty learning communities are discussed in a later section of this chapter.

But a cohort is not a learning community in and of itself. To reach this level requires intentional and disciplined work, as Smith and colleagues (2004) point out:

> The term *learning communities* [refers] to a variety of curricular approaches that intentionally link or cluster two or more courses, often around an interdisciplinary theme or problem, and enroll a common cohort of students. They represent an intentional restructuring of students' time, credit, and learning experiences to build community, enhance learning, and foster connections among students, faculty, and disciplines. At their best, learning communities practice pedagogies of active engagement and reflection. (p. 20)

Experience with the Integrated Model shows the great benefit of a student cohort approach. Cohort instructors work together to discuss and assess student progress as well as to develop interdisciplinary themes that link modules and build connections. A team approach to teaching is easily accomplished with a cohort model. The same teachers with the same students make for collaborative faculty opportunities. Cohorts encourage and facilitate bonds among students and, if done right, with their faculty as well.

Student Work Groups

Within a cohort learning community, small student work groups can add value to the educational and teaching experiences. These intact work groups operate in and outside class using virtual collabo- rative environments for collaboration and cooperation on a variety of assignments and projects. This group approach can help students learn from one another and develop team skills that they will need throughout their academic and work careers. Experience shows that student teams, no matter how large or small, evolve their own group dynamics. They end up not only collaborating on projects but also engaging in interpersonal work on group and individual dynam- ics, which is so important for academic and employment success. Instructors can offer guidance on group organizational matters hav- ing to do with rotating leadership positions, time management, and deliverable deadlines.

Students organize their work groups and set various leadership roles so that tasks are accomplished on time. At times, work groups turn in assignments as a group, and at other times individual assign- ments are required. In all cases, students in work groups have the opportunity to assess themselves and their work-group colleagues so that the instructor knows the level of participation and con- tribution of individuals. Self-evaluations are an important part of work-group activities and are discussed in more detail later in this chapter. These small student work groups can stay intact across concurrent modules during a semester and thus derive produc- tivity efficiencies, which is yet another advantage of the student cohort approach.

Academic Themes

The use of academic themes in an integrated three-year-degree program can be a powerful means for providing focus, linking mod- ules, and helping stakeholders understand the intentionality of the curriculum. Overarching themes can span an entire program of study, adding cohesion to the academic experience. Themes provide the opportunity to better organize the curriculum and allow faculty to introduce related academic activities such as guest lecturers, field trips, and summer reading requirements that reinforce themes as well as speak to traditional module content. Further, an entire semester's curriculum can be organized around a particular idea that falls under a larger umbrella.

Themes that are woven into the fabric of the integrated program can powerfully connect various modules and help students understand the larger pictures associated with not only their current semester learning experiences but with their entire program of study. This is also an opportunity for participating faculty to understand more completely what the three-year program is all about. In this vein, professional learning communities provide learning opportunities for faculty to burst the bonds of their disciplinary silos and embrace a truly interdisciplinary integrated approach to high-quality education. Professional learning communities are discussed in more detail later in this chapter.

Here is an example of an overarching program theme and some yearlong themes from a three-year business administration program:

Overarching Program Theme for All Three Years:
"Student as Leader and Manager"

Year One: "Humanities and the Individual"

Year Two: "Humanities and the Group"

Year Three: "Humanities and the Organization and Community"

Professional Learning Communities

Experience shows that an important hallmark of a successful integrated model is a three-year teaching faculty that comes together in a professional learning community of their own.

The cross-disciplinary, collaborative, and integrative nature of diverse faculty members' contributions to the model cannot be underestimated.

R. DuFour, in his article "What Is a 'Professional Learning Community'" (2004) and in his book with Eaker, *Professional Learning Communities at Work: Best Practices for Enhancing Student Achievement* (1998), speaks to the efficacy of teaching faculty working interdependently. In the blog article "What Is a PLC?" (2008), B. DuFour and R. DuFour say that faculty in a professional learning community work

> to clarify exactly what each student must learn, monitor each student's learning on a timely basis, provide systematic interventions that ensure students receive additional time and support for learning when they struggle, and extend and enrich learning when students have already mastered the intended outcomes.

A very high degree of instructional planning, implementation, and integration adds value to the integrated three-year curriculum. Instructors collaborate and often teach in teams, working closely together on a regular basis to coordinate and integrate student learning experiences and activities. Teaching faculty meet together regularly. Highly involved as a group, teaching faculty discuss student progress, figure out ways to help students overcome hurdles, and coordinate joint projects and assignments. And, yes, they can assess and grade jointly. As a result, mutually reinforced, highly integrated, and purposeful coordinated activities can be woven throughout the entire curriculum.

All faculty members participating in the Integrated Three-Year Program are considered part of a larger team and remain so during the entire academic year. Faculty participants serve as resources and consultants for other instructors and for all students in the program.

This consulting function goes beyond what faculty members do for their own module teaching commitments.

As discussed in Chapter 3, there are integrating experiences after the conclusion of each of the first four semesters, during which working groups of students acquire and synthesize knowledge and skills and see the relevance and relatedness of their learning experiences. The case studies or projects that drive the integrated experiences are collectively selected or created and graded by the interdisciplinary faculty teaching team that taught the students during the just-concluded semester. For year three's yearlong integrating experience, typically one faculty member is responsible for all aspects of the experience, including grading. This person can call for assistance from any three-year faculty teaching that academic year because teaching faculty sign up for an entire year of consulting beyond the module that they are responsible for. There is no reason why a faculty team could not run this yearlong experience.

It is easy to talk about professional learning communities, but putting one together offers a number of challenges. At some institutions, faculty members are not used to working closely with those outside of their discipline to coordinate and create academic learning activities in support of learning outcomes. In fact, the notions of learning outcomes and competencies may be foreign to some, although less so now than in the past. Nevertheless, professional development efforts may need to be provided.

In addition, the pedagogical approaches discussed in the following section may be uncomfortable for some faculty, especially if they have been employing a lecture approach for much of their teaching careers. Finally, some faculty may be resentful if they have been assigned to teach in a three-year program against their will. Resistance and undermining could occur. Experience shows that when the three-year program is supported at the top level of the institutional administration and when teaching in the program is seen as a true mark of distinction, many of these negatives are removed, clearing the way to reach faculty who are motivated to participate in a new educational adventure.

Professional development can consist of a variety of workshops and brief readings that cover the unique features of the Integrated Three-Year Program, active learning and teaching styles, the fundamentals of learning outcomes and competency-based education, ways to assess student progress, and the use of a sophisticated information technology infrastructure along with Web 2.0 strategies. Professional development readings might include Barr and Tagg's (1995) article that places the focus on active student engagement, with instructors serving as guides rather than sages, along with tips on how to engage students in and out of the classroom. The emphasis is on collaborative, cooperative, and problem-based pedagogy. Each instructor has wide latitude with regard to instructional methods. Much of the professional development is on how to leverage virtual collaborative environments in the service of student learning. Faculty get to understand the limitations of the "sage on the stage" teaching approach and the advantages of the "guide on the side" approach.

Ideally, faculty would have release time for professional development, and participation would be rewarded with appropriate accolades noted in their personnel folders. Needless to say, adequate resources to carry out this professional development project will need to be provided. This is why support from the administrative top is so crucial. This kind of support and the many attending issues surrounding it are discussed in Chapter 4.

Active Teaching and Learning in the Learning Paradigm

There are many ways that students learn and teachers teach. This book does not argue that one or another teaching or learning paradigm is better for some students or other students. From experience, the learning paradigm described by Barr and Tagg (1995) and by Tagg (2003) seems to work well with the Integrated Model along with other value-added dimensions to extend the physical classroom beyond space and time and to maximize student learning outcomes. The learning paradigm seems to be a good fit for cohort-based, small-group project approaches and fits nicely with virtual collaboration environments and learning communities. As Barr and Tagg (1995) so aptly phrase it:

> In the Learning Paradigm, learning environments and activities are learner-centered and learner-controlled. They may even be "teacherless." While teachers will have designed the learning experiences and environments students use—often through teamwork with each other and other staff—they need not be present for or participate in every structured learning activity. (p. 11)

Barr and Tagg (1995) and others make a distinction between the instruction paradigm, where teaching and the teacher are central, and the learning paradigm, where learning and learning outcomes are central. In the instruction paradigm, the faculty member's role is mostly as an expert in a particular discipline who delivers knowledge via the lecture mode. In the learning paradigm, the faculty is a learning environment designer. Alternatives to the lecture approach are encouraged and many can be found in Blumberg's *Developing Learner-Centered Teachers: A Practical Guide for Faculty* (2008) and in Weimer's *Learner-Centered Teaching: Five Key Changes to Practice* (2002).

Experience shows that moving away from the straight instructor lecture to other teaching modalities engages students in multiple ways. "Active learning" is an umbrella term for instructional methods that strive to actively engage students in the learning process. Engagement is the key notion here. There are many aspects to active learning. "Collaborative learning" refers to instructional methods where students work together in small groups. "Cooperative learning" refers to group work where common goals are pursued without competition. "Problem-based learning" uses relevant problems or cases to provide context and motivate the learners. Prince (2004) in "Does Active Learning Work? A Review of the Research" and Cooper, Robinson, and Ball (2003) in *Small Group Instruction in Higher Education: Lessons of the Past, Visions of the Future* demonstrate that all these approaches are geared toward student engagement beyond what lecturing can provide.

Svinicki and McKeachie (2010) in their very popular textbook *McKeachie's Teaching Tips: Strategies, Research, and Theory for College and University Teachers* suggest group discussions to promote motivation for learning and to help students articulate and reflect on what they are learning. Group discussions help students to exercise subject-matter thinking and apply newly learned principles. Discussions also help students learn to evaluate their own positions and group members' positions. An evaluation component is a central feature of learning to think critically.

The central idea of active learning is that until students do something with knowledge, they don't store it in long-term memory. Doing something with new knowledge helps to solidify it. In the learning paradigm, the teacher need not be the center of attention. Much learning can go on without constant interaction with a teacher. This is where collaborative, cooperative, and problem-based learning in groups comes into play. As Svinicki and McKeachie (2010) show, there is a great deal of research to support this proposition.

Teachers posing questions to students and students posing questions to teachers and each other is a time-honored way to stimulate active learning in and out of the classroom. Utilizing a virtual collaborative environment is one way to foster questioning even beyond the classroom and can provide a good venue for students to generate questions and answer them for themselves, their classmates, and their teachers.

Of course, active teaching and learning is not exclusive to integrated three-year programs. But when one combines it with student cohorts and their intact student work groups and with curricula based on competency and learning outcomes, the combination provides much synergy.

Virtual Collaborative Environments

Meaningful learning takes time, attention, perseverance, and energy. Learning outcomes and their supporting learning activities can be structured inside and outside the physical classroom in ways that maximize the potential for student success. Learning activities can be extended beyond the classroom walls and time frames by the kind of web-based virtual collaborative environments that are already in use in many distance education programs throughout higher education. These course management systems, in addition to some of the Web 2.0 technologies such as social media networks, can be leveraged into a virtual collaborative environment.

Course Management Systems as Virtual Collaborative Environments

A course management system consists of a Web-based platform that provides space for instructors to post files such as audio and video clips of key learning points they have presented as well as other important electronic artifacts. The system is also used to collect completed assignments. There is typically a facility for students to electronically drop off completed assignments and for instructors to post comments and grades for these completed assignments via a grade book. E-mail and live chat are also features of many course management systems.

Perhaps the most important part of the course management system is the threaded discussions forum, where students and instructors can converse on topics of interest and post and address questions. This is a way to asynchronously advance discussion topics begun but not completed in a face-to-face class session or vice versa. Most course management systems enable the instructor to grade students on their threaded discussion contributions. The course management system is Web-based and available only to those registered for a module or course associated with the particular course management system. Course management systems can also contain group pages that can be assigned to specific sets of students so that teams can take advantage of the collaborative features of the course management system for their own specific work group. This is a semi-private aspect of a course management system within a course management system.

Web 2.0 as a Virtual Collaborative Environment

Web 2.0 is a new generation of Web applications that constitute an infrastructure for dynamic user participation which facilitates user social interaction and widespread collaboration. Two popular examples are Facebook and Twitter. One of the hallmarks of Web 2.0 is user-generated content along with a platform for interactive participation from a wide variety of others. Examples are blogs, wikis, and social networking/sharing sites, media sharing, social bookmarking, collaborative knowledge development, content aggregation and organization, remixing, and mash-ups. In "Web 2.0 and Classroom Research: What Path Should We Take Now?" Greenhow, Robelia, and Hughes (2009) explore and expose the advantages and pitfalls of Web 2.0 for education. Some course management systems already have facilities for wikis and blogs and for connections to social networking sites.

For example, a blog is owned by one user (typically the professor) who creates posts (such as questions, challenges, and files) in reverse chronological order. Each blog post has a comment facility where students can reply. Replies to replies are also allowed. This is similar to threaded discussion forums. Wikis are collaborative websites with multiple pages where multiple users can easily create as well as edit one another's content. Wikis are popular as a collaborative and cooperative virtual space where work-group members can collaborate and create documents in concert. As Bonk (2009) points out in *The World Is Open: How Web Technology Is Revolutionizing Education*, "blogs, wikis, social networks and so much else are Open Source and free for the taking or using."

Thus, one does not have to pay for these added features in course management systems.

In addition, simulations, serious games, and virtual worlds are playing an ever-increasing role in education. Aldrich (2009a), in *Learning Online with Games, Simulations, and Virtual Worlds: Strategies for Online Instruction*, shows that additional dimensions are emerging as valuable pedagogical tools in the education milieu. Educational games and simulations, sometimes called "serious games," can leverage cooperative as well as competitive student behavior. They can involve "play" at the individual as well as group levels. And their pedagogical potential to bring together educational content within social media dimensions has only begun to be appreciated (Aldrich, 2009b).

Scenario without a Course Management System and without Web 2.0

Admittedly, this is a rather extreme scenario, but it is used to make a later point. Students meet together with their instructors in face-to-face classroom sessions. Instructors present new material and go over homework assignment answers. Students ask questions during the class. Instructors use formative and summative evaluations to assess student understanding. There might be some in-class group work, student presentations, and discussion of assignments.

Before the next class meeting, students review class material and prepare by reviewing class notes, doing readings and homework assignments, and maybe collaborating in groups (that is, study groups, project groups) if it is physically possible to get together. Students return to the next class meeting, and the process is repeated again. During the time between classes, students might contact the instructor via e-mail or phone or maybe even attend office hours asking for clarifications or help. They may contact other students in the class for the same things. Homework can be delivered prior to class or at class time. The instructor will need time to assess the homework and to return graded homework and exams.

Scenario with a Course Management System and with Web 2.0

A course management system provides a convenient virtual classroom setting where students can electronically pick up and drop off assignments anytime and from anywhere. They can be immediately alerted about instructor-posted comments and grading if they subscribe to an RSS feed notification. The course management system is a virtual repository where instructors and students can post files (such as videos and documents) for the benefit of the entire class or privately via group pages. But most importantly, it is a place where discussions can be carried on outside the classroom with the entire class or within designated student groups or between student and instructor. These threaded discussion boards contain topics called forums. Inside a forum, the instructor might pose questions or items for research (that is, threads). Students can post replies, and other students and the instructor can post replies to these replies. This allows for in-class conversations, research, writing, and learning to move beyond the walls and the time frame of the physical classroom. Many course management systems have a grading facility so that teachers can log assessments of individual and group discussion contributions.

Much of the same can be accomplished through blogs, where the blog owner creates posts and others reply. Wikis are used for collaborative writing. Group assignments can easily flourish there. The important point is that the use of virtual collaborative environments can help to make more efficient use of student nonclass time by extending the classroom in time and space. All these features are part of highly successful online distance education programs that many universities are very familiar with. Learning to utilize and feel comfortable with the many features of any virtual collaborative environment takes time, energy, and training for both students and faculty alike. The payoffs can be enormous.

The potential for Web 2.0 technologies to transform education is something many scholars are beginning to consider. A new and vibrant three-year degree program would do well to keep a pulse on the educational research in this area. The Greenhow, Robelia, and Hughes (2009) article is a start. Current research can be found in scholarly journals such as the *Journal of Educational Computing Research*.

Student Assessment

Assessment is the glue that binds these many value-added dimensions of integrated three-year programs. After all, any program based on student learning outcomes, which is what the learning paradigm is all about, must assess student progress toward competency achievement. Students have the right to know where they stand at all times, and instructors need to have this information if they are to do their jobs well. Virtual collaborative environments can help provide an infrastructure for instructors to do summative and formative assessments and to let their students know the results. But a virtual collaborative environment is only an infrastructure. It needs content and direction to carry out its tasks effectively.

The corpus of literature on competencies and competency assessment is deep, as many of the titles in the *Assessment Update* series show (http://www.josseybass.com/WileyCDA/WileyTitle/productCd-AU.html). Formative feedback has long been recognized as a central pedagogical technique for furthering knowledge acquisition, improving learning, and motivating learners. Shute's (2008) article "Focus on Formative Feedback" provides a comprehensive review and identifies three categories of feedback factors: task specificity (targeted at errors), content complexity (less informational content), and feedback timing issues. In Chapter 2 of this book, creating the competencies at the program level was only one of the first steps. In Chapter 3, the content of academic plans associated with the modules were shown to provide powerful ways to identify opportunities for formative assessments. It is these plans that form the basis for model syllabi and serve to ensure the alignment of learning experiences and competencies held together with the assessment glue. This is illustrated by Figure 3.3.

One of the distinct advantages of professional learning communities is the way they can provide for multiple perspectives on student assessment. A virtual collaborative environment can contribute in substantive and administrative ways. Having an easy way to grade and comment on student assignments, including threaded discussion forums, makes course management systems an indispensible tool in the teacher's assessment repertoire. Most course management systems have a facility to survey and test students and collect and disseminate their responses both individually and as teams.

Lincoln and Guba in *Naturalistic Inquiry* (1985) describe prolonged engagement and persistent observation as two of three recognized qualitative measures utilized by faculty to assess student progress toward achieving competency mastery. In a cohort-based three-year degree program, teaching faculty members meet regularly throughout the semester to collaborate on joint assignments but also to share their observations of each student. Considerations of academic rigor, social pressures, and the coordination of academic assignments are examples of issues that can be discussed in these meetings. In addition to developing a "collective intelligence" regarding the students, faculty members can team teach, consult with one another, and visit each other's classrooms, thus adding to the development of a thick description assessment.

The techniques of prolonged engagement and persistent observation can be triangulated with the third qualitative assessment technique: nonparticipant observation. Nonparticipant observation can occur during each semester as faculty members teaching in one year of the program observe the performance of students in the other two years of the program.

Students can participate in the assessment process in very direct ways. They can evaluate the levels of participation and quality of contributions of teammates during group projects, including the

very important end-of-semester and yearlong integrating experiences. This is sometimes called "calibrated peer review" and may
use an instructor-generated rubric such as those in Robinson's article "Calibrated Peer Review: An Application to Increase Student
Reading and Writing Skills" (2001).

Student progress is continually evaluated in each module, and
they are thus able to know, on a regular basis, where they stand
with respect to module completion and program-level competency
achievement. Students who finish a module within the module time
frame but who have not achieved one or more program competencies or course-level learning outcomes at the prescribed level do not
receive academic credit for the module until the competency-level
deficiency is remedied. Competency achievement occurs at various stages throughout the curriculum, with achievement at certain
levels of each competency expected throughout the three years.
Students might remain enrolled at the university at no additional
tuition expense until all competencies are achieved.

Walkthrough Perspectives: Students and Teachers

Experience tells us what an integrated three-year program of study
can look like from a student's and a teacher's perspective. What fol-
lows is from the SNHU three-year business administration degree,
but it can be easily modified to fit almost any academic program.

Year-One Activities

Incoming students and current three-year students are assigned a
set of readings, typically a novel, to complete prior to fall freshman
orientation. The readings, and possibly movies and articles, are
chosen by the Three-Year Steering Committee, which is made
up of three-year teaching faculty and administrators. The idea is
to give the incoming students a common academic experience
prior to the start of school and something they can discuss during
orientation sessions. The readings are also covered in one or more

of the modules of year one, semester one. But because returning three-year students are also assigned the same summer readings, a common student connection is made up and down the program year levels. The connections are not only for students. Teaching faculty members are also expected to do the readings and to incorporate them, where applicable, into their semester modules.

1. As part of the admissions process, all prospective three-year students are interviewed by admissions professionals who are conversant with the three-year program, its philosophy, and the requirements for success. Parents are provided with similar information.

2. To prepare for an incoming year-one class, faculty choose an appropriate summer reading book, which is given free to each student in June of their senior year of high school. They are told that the book will be discussed in their classes and at orientation prior to classes.

3. During the previous spring semester, teaching faculty for the fall semester are chosen and meet for professional development and to schedule meetings for the upcoming semester. It is here that participating faculty members discuss and share what they plan to do in their modules and begin to think about joint assignments and cooperative ventures. Summer is a good time for exchanges about these things.

4. The Three-Year Integrated Program Steering Committee consisting of teaching faculty, staff, and administrators meets on a regular basis to conduct strategic planning for the program and programmatic evaluations. It is at this level that integrating themes are solicited, vetted, and chosen. The steering committee is active in recruiting faculty to teach in the Integrated Program. The program's mission statement is typically revisited each year. See Appendix G for an example of a mission statement.

5. Incoming students are connected on a three-year program so-cial network site, such as Facebook, so that they get to know one another prior to meeting face to face in a summer campus orientation. The program administrator is also on the Facebook page.

6. Students receive an e-mail in the summer with information about the summer readings and the computer hardware and software that they will need for their university career. Laptop computers are required in the program as well as productivity software.

7. Students arrive on campus during the regular freshman orientation and participate in all four-year student orientation activities as well as those specifically for three-year students. They may have a laptop orientation with an introduction to the virtual collaborative environment so that they can start using it on the first day of classes.

8. Three-year students are divided into cohorts with an attempt to balance the cohorts by size, gender, and commuter and on-campus students. The cohorts are remixed at the start of the second semester.

9. Teaching faculty begin to meet on a regular basis to plan and so-lidify joint assignments, evaluate, and discuss student progress. In addition, planning for the end-of-semester Integrating Experience case study commences.

10. Classes begin and student cohorts are welcomed into their modules. Connecting themes for the semester and year are discussed with students. It is clear to students as the semester progresses that all their teachers are meeting on a regular basis because each teacher knows what the others are doing, is aware of any snags, and is cognizant of individual student progress as well as general cohort progress in all modules. Joint assignments are another sign that instructors are collaborating. It is common for an instructor to open a class by asking what the students

did in the module preceding the one they are sitting in. Depending upon their response, the teacher can make comments and even provide insights that not only demonstrate a working knowledge of the semester curriculum but also indicate that faculty teams are meeting on a regular basis and that concurrent module content is known to all the teaching faculty.

11. Students quickly get attuned to the virtual collaborative environment and begin posting replies to instructor-generated questions—inside and outside of class. They soon begin to formulate and post questions of their own and replies to one another's questions. The summer reading book is addressed in at least one module and likely more than one.

12. Group work is a hallmark of the Integrated Program. Typically, small work groups of three to five students are formed at the start of a semester within a cohort. Often, these work groups are the same across the various modules. Students are told to organize their work groups so that tasks are accomplished on time and that various leadership roles are settled. Sometimes the work group turns in a completed assignment as a group, and sometimes individual assignments are called for. In all cases, students in work groups have the opportunity to assess themselves and their work group partners so that the teacher knows the level of participation and contribution of group members.

13. Students immediately begin to communicate and work with one another through the virtual collaborative environment. The course management system is a place for students to receive announcements from instructors via RSS feed notifications signaling posts to discussion board forums. Students are expected to check their e-mail and their course management system accounts regularly during the day. Student teams use course management system group pages to collaborate on assignments and research, and they can use wikis to collectively create documents.

14. Another hallmark of the program is the use of e-portfolios. As Cambridge (2010) discusses in *Eportfolios for Lifelong Learning and Assessment,* this is a way for students to post their most creative work while they build a portfolio for assessment and for future job seeking. Although laptop computers used to be the Internet appliance of choice, many students now use iPads and other tablet computers along with Web-enabled cell phones (that is, smartphones) to connect to their virtual classroom.

15. Faculty and the steering committee select next summer's readings.

16. At the conclusion of the regular semester modules, students enter the integrating experience module phase, where each cohort breaks into small work groups. These groups receive a case or project and instructions from their module teaching faculty and begin their collaboration, which culminates in presentations and write-ups one week later. Faculty grading begins as students leave for their semester break.

17. Students who fail to make adequate competency progress by the end of the first semester are given help and remedial work during the semester break. They are then assessed at the start of the following semester by their teaching faculty.

18. At the start of year one, semester two, student cohort membership is reconstituted, although there is nothing sacred about doing this.

19. Semester two is much like semester one for students, faculty, and administrators, and it too culminates in an end-of-semester integrating experience—and then summer break.

Year-Two Activities

1. Over the summer, the second- and third-year students will also read the common book assigned to the incoming first-year students.

2. Year two is very much like year one. Student cohort member-
    ship is reconstituted at the start of each semester. There are
    integrating experiences at the end of each semester.

Year-Three Activities

1. During year three, students are able to take some elective
    courses with four-year degree students. This allows the three-
    year students to branch out and study areas of particular interest.

2. The fall semester begins with the students participating in a
    year-long integrating experience referred to as their "senior
    project."

3. The senior project is a form of applied management/
    experiential learning that is integrated within a module in the
    form of an organized, thoughtful, and meaningful project. Des-
    ignated teams of two to five students are matched with agencies,
    organizations, or business enterprises that have specific needs
    related to the content of the students' curriculum. The teams
    perform the needed service, which is research based, drawing
    upon their academic knowledge, new and old. At the end, each
    team provides a tangible final product or deliverable as a result
    of its efforts (items 3–11: Painchaud, 2010).

4. Some of the objectives of this yearlong integrating experience
    are for students to gain practical experience in project man-
    agement, integrating academics and business practices. Ad-
    ditional knowledge and insight are gained in the areas of
    interrelationships of human assets, decision-making impact,
    management techniques, and functions such as planning, or-
    ganizing, leading, and controlling, which assist in attaining the
    desired outcomes.

5. Here is how teams are established. Students are assessed
    by several criteria, including but not limited to personality,
    discipline, aptitude, past integrating team membership, and

communications skills among other items. Teams are constituted based upon these factors, with typically four students per team.

6. Projects must be selected. Teaching faculty have already solicited and screened worthy causes and projects. Abstracts of the clients' projects are distributed to the student teams. Using assessments of their talents, skill, and ability, along with sincere interest and even passion for a project, teams rank order the project candidates. The yearlong integrating experience faculty director reviews the rankings and assigns the projects based on several criteria such as desire, skills, abilities, talent, fit, and sometimes input from faculty colleagues and others.

7. Once teams and their respective projects have been assigned, the team has an initial meeting with the client. Basic parameters are established regarding each team's designated liaison between team and client through whom all communication will flow. In addition, this initial meeting will settle on frequency of contact for the fall semester, guidelines for interaction, arrangements for site visits, and coordination of data collection, among other things.

8. The first semester is devoted to background work including but not limited to current issues analyses of the client's organization (such as history and overview); research on the issues that the client currently faces; and the development of an action plan which the team will work to accomplish during the second semester.

9. The early part of the second semester of year three is when the teams do the research and work on the deliverable for their clients. Team deliverables are finalized toward the end of the second semester, when they give presentations to their clients and to the university community. Teams are graded on their deliverables and presentations.

10. Clients have responsibilities. They are expected to provide information, guidance, and parameters regarding the team projects. Since teams are modeled after self-directed project management teams, they should be making good progress with little prodding from the client.

11. The outcome of the yearlong integrating experience is that students are able to demonstrate the acquisition and applications of theories and concepts that support many of the program-level competencies. A series of graded deliverables is scheduled throughout the academic year, and students in teams are asked to assess their teammates with regard to participation, contribution, and cooperation among other dimensions.

Recap

Kuh and colleagues (2010) in their book *Student Success in College: Creating the Conditions That Matter* show that a rigorous culminating experience for seniors is almost always a salutary endeavor. The forum provided for the presentation of the results of these experiences is a venue to reward "outstanding academic performance and reinforce high expectations for all students" (p. 190). The active learning, assessment and feedback, and collaboration among students are important factors in student development and help lead to student success in college, which in turn can lead to greater student retention. The value-added dimensions discussed in this chapter can go a long way toward supporting a competency-based education and ultimately student success.

7

Comparing Three-Year Degree Models

At this point in the book, the reader has an appreciation for the Integrated, Competency-Based Model, the change challenges that it represents, and the proof of concept. With these things in mind, we can now make a more detailed comparison of the most common three-year-degree models in use today. This was initiated in Table 1.1 but can now be elaborated on here.

Specifically, the different approaches are compared across a set of seven program-level attributes. These program attributes assist in framing the similarities as well as the differences between the models.

This is an important exercise to undertake because decision makers will want to carefully weigh the pros and cons of these various models. Although this book advocates the Integrated Model, the advantages to the others ought to be made clear. The tables on the following pages compare the attributes of the three models of three-year-degree programs.

View of the Curriculum

Accelerated Curriculum Model	Prior Learning Model	Integrated Curriculum Model
Curriculum advancements are marginal and incremental.	Curriculum credit for prior learning is awarded through a variety of methods.	Curriculum advancements are breakthrough.

In the Accelerated Curriculum Model, any curriculum advancements are viewed as incremental and/or discrete. Using this approach, traditional courses are delivered in an organized and more or less sequential manner so that students are assured of being able to complete their program of study in thirty-six months rather than forty-eight months.

In the Prior Learning Model, students typically receive credit for completing a certified curriculum such as Advanced Placement coursework. Another means of credit attainment, particularly for nontraditional students, is the development of a portfolio that documents or demonstrates a student's prior learning. The College Level Examination Program (CLEP) is another way that students can receive college credit. Students receive credit by passing an examination that typically focuses on content areas required in the first two years of study.

In the Integrated Curriculum Model, curriculum advances require more intensive and, in some cases, sweeping structural changes. So for example, curriculum is designed or redesigned and delivered so that students can achieve program-level competencies and desired learning outcomes. In this approach, some content areas may be delivered more time intensively, and others are achieved through many curriculum-related activities over the length of the entire academic year and in several different modules.

Curriculum Restructuring or Redesign

Accelerated Curriculum Model	Prior Learning Model	Integrated Curriculum Model
No integration of curriculum—the focus remains on seat time.	No integration of curriculum—yet the importance of prior learning experiences is recognized.	Integration of curriculum—the focus is on learning and the demonstration of competencies.

One clear advantage of an Accelerated Curriculum Model is that very little curriculum change is needed. Historical practices are maintained as students continue to honor the metrics of credit hours and seat time. Class structure remains the same in that courses are delivered in familiar patterns, such as semesters, quarters, eight-week sessions, and six-week time blocks. However, designated administrators need to oversee the course delivery schedule more closely. Even with thoughtful administrative oversight, students may fall out of the planning cycle of course offerings and thus experience difficulty completing the program of study in three years. As an accelerated program gains scale, students will have more choices and opportunities for completing the program within the desired three years.

In a Prior Learning Model, emphasis is rightly placed on having a system or an administrative process in place so that students can seamlessly request credit for courses, certificates, and other formally recognized academic experiences. No integration or redesign of the curriculum is required for a Prior Learning Model. Rather, what is required is a system that meets the needs of the particular college or university and one that has been developed and supported through the appropriate campus governance mechanisms.

For an Integrated, Competency-Based Curriculum Model, the curriculum needs to be restructured or redesigned, guided by the notion that all learning must contribute to the demonstration of one or more of the program competencies. In its design and implementation, the integrated, competency-based curriculum shifts faculty emphasis away from seat time and contact hours and focuses instead on being student-centered. Where appropriate, the modules are interdisciplinary or intradisciplinary. One example of this approach in action is the semester-ending integrating academic experiences, in which teams of students work collaboratively as a means of summarizing, synthesizing, and advancing their newly acquired skills and knowledge.

As previously mentioned, the English faculty were able to deliver the foundations for public speaking in the two three-credit English modules. Then due to the high degree of integration of the first-year curriculum, students' public speaking skills and abilities were reinforced, demonstrated, and evaluated throughout the first year. Academic plans provide the means for faculty to see and understand the totality of the curriculum. As Gardiner (1994) notes, most curricula lack focus and often do not produce the intended results due to the absence of structure. Academic plans provide the structure that allows skills and knowledge to be developed and reinforced over multiple modules and over the entire year. This is an example of a curriculum breakthrough that allows for numerous opportunities for students to apply and practice the skills and knowledge that are intentionally delivered by the teaching faculty.

Administrative Needs for the Program

Accelerated Curriculum Model	Prior Learning Model	Integrated Curriculum Model
The focus is on *management* activities and fits the current administrative/ business model.	The focus is on administrative review and related activities required to certify prior learning.	The focus is on systems changes and *leadership* activities and requires a new view of the administrative/ business model.

When an Accelerated Curriculum Model is launched, attention is given to the related management activities required for seamless integration with current administrative practices. Specifically, the emphasis is on ensuring that little if any disruption occurs in managing the Accelerated Curriculum Program with respect to the entrenched institutional business practices. So, for example, all tuition and other institutional fees remain unchanged as students progress through their program of study. In some cases, institutions may decide not to charge tuition for the final ten courses, in effect charging students for only three years of tuition even though they have completed forty three-credit courses.

To implement the Prior Learning Model, a system must be developed to facilitate student utilization of the approach. A designated individual or office must provide oversight and support, thus ensuring that students' prior learning is reviewed in a timely manner.

This process must also include mechanisms to take into account prior learning, such as on-the-job experience. Institutions often need to designate appropriate personnel to evaluate the students' work/career portfolios.

For an institution to successfully implement an Integrated Curriculum Model, leadership is required from the senior academic officer as well as from the president. Conceiving and implementing this model requires that administrative leaders possess the will to break old patterns, such as traditional class meeting times and lecture-formatted classes that are faculty-centered rather than student-centered. Program-level administrators need to work with teaching faculty to develop module-level academic plans that map back to the major module strategies and to identify the activities that contribute to the development of one or more of the program competencies. Teaching faculty will be challenged by their classrooms being open to other faculty and administrators, and this shift may be more difficult at institutions where faculty have grown accustomed to classrooms being private sanctuaries.

Enrollment Strategy Approach

Accelerated Curriculum Model	Prior Learning Model	Integrated Curriculum Model
Institution may need to cut profit margins in order to compete for new enrollments.	Institution generates little if any revenue from the review of prior-learning content but attracts new enrollments.	Institution protects profit margins and competes in a new space that brings in new and different students.

Although different institutions have their own reasons for implementing an accelerated program, it is clear that many of these new programs are appearing as a result of external pressure. Public calls have been made by third parties, such as the Rhode Island legislature (State of Rhode Island, 2009) and various state governors, to offer a solution for the escalating cost of postsecondary education. The strategy when implementing this model is to attract more of the same kind of students that the institution already attracts while also improving student retention.

The Prior Learning Model is best viewed as a service strategy approach. Although the institution generates minimal revenue from the act of recognizing prior learning or accepting prior credits, one motive to pursue this approach is mission fit. Another clear benefit for an institution with a reputation for a well-developed prior learning program is the likelihood that more of these qualified students will be attracted to apply; with each admitted student comes the potential of new multiyear revenues.

The motive to implement an Integrated Curriculum Model is to compete in new and uncontested space within one's institutional peer group. The new curriculum model attracts both students and faculty who share a common interest in learning and innovation. Faculty see the opportunities that come with a collaborative, student-centered classroom, and potential students are attracted by a program and class environment that both challenges and supports their learning aspirations. It is important to note that these students can represent a new demographic for the institution; with this new segment comes a new revenue stream. This last point addresses a common criticism of new degree programs, that the new programs cannibalize the existing student pool.

Leadership View

Accelerated Curriculum Model	Prior Learning Model	Integrated Curriculum Model
Institutional leaders choose to resist change, preferring traditional delivery models and cost structures.	Institutional leaders view the process of prior learning as an administrative activity.	Institutional leaders see opportunities that come with embracing change and implementing new delivery models that promote new revenue streams.

One of the trappings of postsecondary education has been the remarkable stability that the enterprise enjoyed for most of the twentieth century. Consequently, the notion of having to consider issues that come with deep change was avoided. As a result, institutional leaders have resisted significant change, remaining wedded to traditional delivery models and cost structures. The last twenty years have been anything but serene with the advent of the Internet and portable learning technologies. In addition to a difficult economy, institutional leaders find themselves facing new challenges that could not have been conceived of just a few decades ago. Some will view the Accelerated Curriculum Model as a smart innovation that looks to involve leadership and addresses the cries from critics for change. Yet in reality, the implementation of this model is merely a management tactic requiring little if any true leadership action.

The Prior Learning Model, for most institutions, will not represent a departure from administrative practices and day-to-day activities. The model is well-known and requires little managerial effort to put in place. The challenge of this approach is that the review and certification of portfolios can become a labor-intensive and even an overwhelming process as more and more students seek to take advantage of this approach.

For institutions to successfully embrace and implement an Integrated Curriculum Model, leadership will be required from the highest levels within the organization. In any successful change initiative, a sense of urgency must be articulated in order for others to get behind and support the proposed project. Institutions that remain insulated from the current realities of the marketplace will be less likely to feel a need to embrace substantial curriculum changes. On the other hand, leaders at institutions that are tuition-driven who have experienced increased pressures from the for-profit higher education sector will have a keen interest in developing an Integrated Curriculum Model regardless of institutional type.

Cost Structure

Accelerated Curriculum Model	Prior Learning Model	Integrated Curriculum Model
Degree path (course work) is faster—yet delivery costs are similar or the same, and in some cases the institution waives the revenue of the final ten courses.	Degree path is faster in that students receive credit for up to ten courses (some institutions even permit more), thus saving tuition expense and time.	Degree path is different and faster—and delivery costs are significantly reduced.

Programs that choose to pursue the Accelerated Curriculum Model seem to fall into one of two categories. We offer a word of caution to schools that choose to pursue the Accelerated Model because the effects of the pricing decision on either end of the continuum could be far-reaching. Some institutions facilitate a process in which students complete a 120-credit-hour degree program in three years and do not charge students for the fourth year of tuition. These institutions incur four years of course delivery costs but reap only three years' worth of tuition. Other institutions allow students to complete the forty courses in three years, but they charge full tuition for every course (thus maintaining the current revenue model).

The Prior Learning Model provides an opportunity for students to reap financial gains if they can meet the institutional criteria. In addition to financial savings, the students will also save time that might have been lost if they had attended a different institution. For students who qualify, this model may be the most attractive and prudent.

For the Integrated Curriculum Model, the degree path is different from the traditional four-year structure. The Integrated Curriculum Model is indeed faster in that students finish in six rather than eight semesters. The redesign of the curriculum also substantially reduces the delivery costs for the institution, thus making it more financially feasible for the institution to pass along the savings to the students participating in the program. However, implementing the Integrated Curriculum Model requires funds to be targeted for professional development and curriculum development; depending on the scale of change being sought, the costs to the institution could be fairly significant. Some may wonder about the institution losing the fourth year of tuition. As long as the institution's annual enrollment targets are met or exceeded, a new revenue stream will have been successfully established.

Savings for Students and Families

Accelerated Curriculum Model	Prior Learning Model	Integrated Curriculum Model
No change in the continued rising costs of postsecondary education—in most cases, little or no savings passed on to families.	If students qualify, they can save time and financial resources.	Key shift in the way postsecondary education is organized and delivered, with savings passed on to families.

Depending on the institutional approach to the Accelerated Curriculum Model, students may save a small amount of tuition dollars or as much as a year's worth of tuition. What students gain regardless of the institution's financial decisions is time. Students are able to enter the workplace a year early in order to begin their careers. With no structural changes made to the curriculum, however, legitimate criticism may be levied that no value-added, outcome-driven change has occurred that benefits the student and society in any meaningful way. Indeed, opponents of this model have already pointed out with disapproval that students have to complete six or seven courses per semester in order to graduate in three years.

Participation in an accelerated program will also prove challenging for students who are working more and more hours year round in order to pay for their education. So on one hand, the accelerated model is attractive for a number of reasons. Yet ironically participation in an accelerated program may require students to work fewer hours, thus forcing them to take on more debt.

The Prior Learning Model provides real value to both the institutions that offer the program and the students who can take advantage of the opportunity. As the number of nontraditional students returning to the classroom increases, the demand for prior learning programs will surely grow. What remains to be seen is whether the Prior Learning Model will be better suited to traditional nonprofit institutions or for-profit institutions. This model may indeed prove to offer nonprofit institutions some advantage over their for-profit counterparts.

With the Integrated Curriculum Model, a restructuring that focuses on the student demonstration of a set of competencies ensures that the academic experience will be outcomes-driven. Students, families, and employers all resonate with the notion that the academic experience begins with the end in mind. The redesign explained in Chapter 2 saves both delivery costs for the institution and tuition for the student while providing the student with a thoughtfully designed educational experience.

Recap

The Accelerated Curriculum Model is the most prevalent three-year-degree program in the American higher education landscape today. More than twelve were launched in the fall of 2010, bringing the number of Accelerated Programs to more than thirty-five nationally with many more set to commence in the fall of 2011 (see Appendix A). Given the design and implementation needs of accelerated programs, it is not surprising that this approach has become a significant option for institutions attempting to demonstrate that they are offering a "new" educational experience with a price incentive for students. However, there may be no real tuition savings for students or cost savings for institutions. Unfortunately, for the institutions that offer this type of degree pathway, it is usually a signal that they are unable or unwilling to embrace the real systemic change that is being called for and is needed in American higher education today.

The Integrated Curriculum Model requires significant effort to design and to implement, yet the benefits of the endeavor make it eminently worthwhile. Intentionally designing and implementing a curriculum around a set of competencies allows for the shift away from the seat-time trap. Measuring outcomes provides a level of accountability that key stakeholders of the academy have sought for many years. This model can be successfully implemented across most disciplines and does not sacrifice the general education component of the curriculum.

Chapter 8 provides answers to frequently asked questions about design, implementation, and other areas of interest to faculty, students, and their families.

Stakeholders' Questions and Answers

A s explained in Chapter 4, for any change to be successful, especially one with the potential to significantly impact an organization, it is essential that the people most affected by the change understand it. The more significant the change, the more critical this understanding is in order to gain broad-based support within the organization. A vision statement and elevator statement can help those leading the change effort and their team members communicate and reinforce the vision to internal and external stakeholders and the rest of the community. This chapter addresses typical questions that university administrators and faculty and government officials might have about the Three-Year Integrated Model. Though explained in more detail in other chapters of the book, these concise answers will help you strongly and clearly articulate the model to others.

Why does the current four-year undergraduate-degree model need to change?

There are good reasons why many experts are calling for fundamental change in the way American higher education is structured.

A primary driver continues to be the failing cost structures of the enterprise. Although some university leaders have made incremental cost improvements in recent years, it is quite clear that many families will not be able to afford tuition increases that oftentimes have been two and three times greater than the annual rate of inflation. Zemsky, Wegner, and Massy (2005) call for fundamental change; for example, they have suggested that a state such as California embrace a three-year model for all of its institutions, changing its system. George Keller (2008) noted that one significant improvement to the cost of colleges and universities would be the introduction of three-year degrees. We believe that three-year degrees will continue to grow in number as more and more families demand cost-sensitive alternatives for the attainment of a bachelor's degree. The Integrated Three-Year-Degree Model can provide significant financial relief for students and their sponsors while providing reduced delivery costs for the institution. Financial considerations are introduced in Chapter 1 and addressed in more detail in Chapter 5. Integrated programs can offer 120 credits without diluting academic integrity.

What institutions are most likely to adopt the Integrated Three-Year-Degree Model?

First adopters will likely be small colleges and universities because they are the largest segment of institutions across the United States. For some public institutions, change will likely be as a result of state legislative action, as recently seen in Rhode Island and Florida. Large public and private universities may also choose to make a three-year-degree option available to students, although this segment will likely be decidedly slower to embrace this option. Private institutions, especially tuition-driven ones, will see the three-year degree as an opportunity to attract additional enrollments by being responsive to society's needs. In particular, these institutions will want to give consideration to the Integrated Three-Year Model. In this era of financial uncertainty, the potential for the adoption of three-year-degree programs appears to be quite significant. While the top 10–20 percent of four-year degree-granting institutions will likely remain fairly insulated from the need to change structurally, that will not be the case for many of the remaining institutions that represent both public and private nonprofit colleges and universities. This was addressed in Chapters 1 and 7.

Is the Integrated Three-Year-Degree Program appropriate for every type of student?

No, it's not appropriate for every student because such a program requires some level of maturity and the willingness to be actively involved in one's education. Certainly, academically talented and motivated students who did well in high school are prime candidates for an integrated three-year program. Because the program is results oriented, it may also be an attractive and appropriate option for bright students who, due to traditional seat-time education based on the lecture approach, were average performers in high school. However, traditional college students who wait until the second or third year to declare a major or those following highly prescriptive curriculum requirements would not benefit from the three-year approach.

Doesn't an academic program of study that delivers a bachelor's degree in six semesters have to compromise academic quality?

Careful attention to competency construction and structuring can ensure that all of a four-year degree's 120 credits of content and competencies can be covered in six semesters. Learning takes time, and some things take longer than other things. But this book demonstrates that a high-quality bachelor's degree in six semesters is eminently doable. Chapters 2 and 3 address this in great detail.

Reworking a four-year degree into a three-year degree requires constant attention to competency attainment and outcome demonstration, which as a result frees up significant space within the curriculum. Chapter 3 shows how the public speaking requirement in a four-year course can be spread throughout a number of three-year modules, thus eliminating the need for a stand-alone public speaking three-year module.

A broad-based longitudinal study focused on quality of education would surely settle the question.

Isn't the Integrated Three-Year-Degree Program simply a four-year program squeezed into three?

The Integrated Three-Year-Degree Program is designed to provide an outcomes-focused and competency-based academic experience for the learner. The Accelerated Degree Model offers little if any curriculum redesign for the learner. In fact, students complete the same courses offered in the four-year format. The only difference is that they complete the 120 credits more rapidly by taking courses at night, on weekends, during summers, or online, in an effort to complete their degree in thirty-six rather than forty-eight months. This is why accelerated programs are sometimes referred to as compressed programs. They are a standard program of study offered more rapidly with little if any cost savings to the institution.

An integrated program of study offers students a redesigned curriculum that provides student-centered learning experiences. Students can complete their program study in six semesters rather than eight because modules are designed so that students demonstrate outcomes and achieve competencies that demonstrate the acquisition of knowledge and skills. An integrated program holds learning rather than seat time as the constant. Chapters 1, 2, 3, and 7 address seat time.

———————

Isn't the Integrated Three-Year-Degree Program just a technical degree with few, if any, general education and liberal arts requirements?

All of the general education and liberal arts requirements in a four-year program can be included in a three-year program. As part of the key competencies essential to an integrated program, students are required to participate in course modules that focus in whole or in part on the program's philosophical, ethical, literary, and artistic traditions. Whether a year-one, semester-one module or summer reading on art history and the humanities, history, classic literary texts, Western and Eastern philosophical traditions, science and the environment, or communications, students are encouraged to confront timeless questions and encounter the great conversations of literature and art history across centuries, generations, and cultures. Three-year students should be expected to demonstrate proficiency in disinterested, skeptical inquiry in the best traditions of higher learning and active citizenship. These and other aspects are addressed in Chapters 2 and 3.

———————

Do integrated three-year-degree programs cost the institution more to deliver than traditional four-year programs?

An integrated three-year-degree program does not cost institutions more to deliver than a four-year program does. In fact, the delivery costs for these three-year programs are less. This is because of the programs' design, which distributes and integrates some academic content into three-year modules that in the four-year programs is delivered in discrete courses. Academic credit is awarded when students demonstrate competency. An example is incorporating the content and requirements of a traditional public speaking course into each academic experience. Students are taught the foundations of public speaking by their faculty experts as part of their two first-year required English modules. Faculty members in the remaining first-year modules and throughout the entire program build upon this work by requiring oral presentations that meet the requirements established by the English faculty. This approach incurs no additional institutional expenses and has the added benefit of reinforcing the importance of public speaking ability by infusing it throughout the curriculum.

A second key design feature is a credit-bearing weeklong integrating experience at the end of each semester during the first two years. Students are placed in new learning teams and are given a comprehensive case or project that is aligned with the semester's curriculum. These academic experiences challenge the students to apply and advance their knowledge of theories and concepts while allowing the faculty to assess student progress on a number of competencies that were the primary focus of the semester. The faculty members teaching in each of these semesters design and deliver these integrating experiences as part of their teaching responsibilities.

In the third year, students also take a yearlong team-based experiential-learning project akin to an internship. Students work under the supervision of a senior faculty member to carry out research-based projects for agencies, organizations, or business enterprises that have specific needs related to the content of a particular course. During the year, students interact on a regular basis with representatives of these entities as they conduct research, develop actions plans to address their needs, and present their finding in formal presentations. Although some marginal costs are associated with these features, typically these expenses include only modest stipends to faculty teaching in the program and coordinating the integrating and experiential learning experiences. Chapter 3 addresses this in detail.

The bottom line is that the Integrated Three-Year-Degree Program is delivered without the institution incurring any significant additional delivery costs. In fact, done right, there can be institutional savings. This is the primary reason that allows the institution to pass savings directly on to the students and their families. Chapter 5 explains how this is possible.

Don't integrated three-year-degree programs ultimately mean that institutions will have less revenue?

There is no reason that offering an integrated three-year-degree program will necessarily result in a loss of revenue to the institution. By design, an integrated program reduces institutional delivery costs, and these savings can be passed on to students. So if enrollment targets are achieved, there should be no loss of annual tuition revenue. Similarly, there will be no loss of room and board fees that would have been generated by students residing in on-campus housing for the fourth year if these beds are filled by non-three-year students. As would be the case at an institution offering no three-year programs, as long as enrollment and housing targets are achieved, there is no loss of annual revenue for the institution. Financial considerations are introduced in Chapter 1 and addressed in more detail in Chapter 5.

Will students enrolled in an integrated three-year-degree program be cheated in their majors by not being exposed to as much academic content as four-year students?

Nothing in the design of an integrated three-year-degree program will diminish academic content in a student's major or in any other aspect of the student's curriculum. Because the focus is on competencies that are composed of knowledge and skills, the transformation of a four-year curriculum into an integrated three-year curriculum guarantees that these competencies are addressed by the kinds of analyses and resulting curriculum redesign shown in Chapters 2 and 3.

———————

Don't students enrolled in an integrated three-year-degree program lose out on opportunities to participate in extracurricular and co-curricular activities, including intercollegiate athletics, during their college years?

Experience shows that students enrolled in an integrated three-year-degree program are as engaged in college life as their four-year counterparts. There is no difference when it comes to their ability to take advantage of the full range of undergraduate opportunities outside the classroom. Experience shows that three-year students participate in a wide variety of campus clubs and organizations, often serving in key leadership positions. They are active members of fraternities and sororities, honor societies, and dance teams. They serve as student ambassadors, resident assistants, and orientation leaders. They successfully compete on intercollegiate athletic teams, play intramural sports, and find time to volunteer in their communities. Many also work one or more jobs as they complete their education.

The three-year model does not hinder or prevent students from fully participating in extracurricular and co-curricular activities, including intercollegiate sports. In fact, the program design recognizes the importance of these kinds of opportunities. Weekly schedules include one full day off from classes and course times that accommodate practice times for student athletes. As would be true for any undergraduate student, effectively managing time is the key to successfully balancing academic and social life. The evidence is that three-year students are able to strike the necessary balance.

Of course, because they attend for three years, these students do not get to participate in a fourth year. But this does not seem to diminish the quality of what they get out of their extracurricular and co-curricular activities. This issue is addressed in Chapter 5.

Are students enrolled in an integrated three-year-degree program prepared to enter the workforce or go on to graduate school after earning their degrees?

Much has been written about the readiness of college graduates to enter the workforce. Often cited is their lack of effective written and oral communication skills, their inability to problem solve, and their difficulty in working collaboratively and resolving conflict. How then can completing an undergraduate degree one year earlier not exacerbate these weaknesses? And what about the maturity level of students graduating in three years? Beyond their academic preparation, are they truly ready to enter the workforce or begin graduate studies? These are valid questions.

Students completing an integrated, competency-based three-year-degree program have demonstrated in a variety of ways, including performance on nationally standardized examinations and assessment of student portfolios and other work products, that they have indeed acquired the necessary knowledge, skills, and competencies to successfully begin their careers or enroll in graduate programs. The yearlong experiential learning projects in the third year of the program play a key role in their preparation, as is shown in Chapter 3. It is truly a transformative experience, and data collected over the years from employers confirms that these graduates are both academically and emotionally prepared. This is explored in some detail in Chapter 5.

What teaching styles and approaches are best suited for integrated three-year-degree programs?

Any program that subscribes to the learning paradigm minimizes the lecture approach. Certainly, stand-up instructor lectures have their place in the education milieu. But active learning requires much more of students than passive listening, especially in an age where students actively interact with one another online and contribute content regularly to Facebook and Twitter and other social media. In such a program, the faculty's predilection is for team-based projects and activities where students can learn from one another with the guidance of the instructor. Naturally, there will be a certain amount of book learning involved. But faculty members find that actively engaging students in meaningful applications and extensions of their book learning is a sure way to effectively promote competency achievement. Students love to interact with one another, and the more that faculty can leverage their natural social inclinations in the service of learning, the better for everyone involved. Encouraging students to use virtual collaborative environments to their maximum is a way of more effectively engaging students in the learning process. Think student-centered, project-based, inquiry-based learning approaches as shown in Chapters 3 and 6. Let them think it's all fun and games in the pursuit of serious goals.

What kinds of additional support and resources do faculty need to be effective teachers in an integrated three-year-degree program?

Three-year-program faculty need several kinds of additional support. Integrated three-year programs are based on competencies and learning outcomes. It behooves teaching faculty to understand, at the very least, the rudiments of the learning paradigm. Professional development can help lecture-based faculty members move to a more student-centered learning approach. In addition, some faculty need to learn how to effectively use virtual collaborative environments provided by course management systems along with other social media facilities. Some faculty may need support and encouragement to work together in a professional learning community to carry out the program. Most importantly, faculty will need professional development about formative and summative assessment in the context of a fast-paced curriculum where seat time is not sacrosanct and the classroom has been extended in time and space. It is likely that an institution's instructional support office or its center for teaching excellence could provide support and resources to teaching faculty. Faculty issues are addressed in Chapter 3.

In an integrated three-year program, what happens if a student does not demonstrate competency achievement by the end of a module? By the end of a semester?

This is not an insurmountable problem, although it can be a challenge. In these cases, the instructors and the student must meet to develop an immediate plan of action. From experience, this plan can be carried out by the student between semesters or over the summer. Certainly, if a student fails to achieve in one or more of the competencies, then she or he cannot continue in the three-year-degree program. Mapping between three-year modules and four-year courses can facilitate a smooth transition into the four-year curriculum so that the student does not need to drop out of school or transfer elsewhere. This issue is covered in Chapter 3.

Is an integrated three-year model just the American version of the Bologna agreement?

An integrated three-year model is different from the Bologna agreement. One of the major roles of the Bologna agreement is to harmonize the educational systems in Europe so that students can move more effortlessly across borders in order to study in different countries. Although many Europeans can and do earn their bachelor's degree in three years, it is important to note that these students have participated in a system that requires thirteen years of elementary and secondary education; examples include the United Kingdom, Germany, and Italy. Chapter 1 includes the details of three-year degrees in a global context that includes Europe, India, and Southeast Asia.

The Three-Year University

This book is about how an integrated three-year-degree program can be created from an existing four-year program without the loss of academic quality and with significant student and institutional savings. The Integrated Model is the only one of the three three-year models that can do this, but pulling it off is challenging. It requires academic leaders to rethink the standard higher education course/credit/seat-time paradigm and be willing to exercise leadership to create an atmosphere for change in their institutions. This is not an easy task but one that is essential for the very survival of many institutions. It is also necessary to ensure that college students are gaining the knowledge and skills that will meet their and society's current and future needs.

This chapter discusses some of the most recent challenges colleges and universities are facing and how the Integrated Three-Year Model can help address them. The book closes with thoughts on what it would take to scale up the Integrated Program Model to encompass a school within a university or even the entire university itself.

Questions about Achieving Learning Outcomes

At the start of 2011, four related events brought a lot more attention to the challenges facing higher education and required colleges and universities to respond. A new book questioning how much college students are actually learning during the time spent earning their undergraduate degrees was published. In his State of the Union address, President Barack Obama called for a renewed commitment to lead the world in the proportion of U.S. citizens earning a college degree. The Lumina Foundation for Education proposed a degree-qualification framework describing what students should know when they graduate from college. And the Association of American Colleges and Universities released a statement supporting the Lumina Foundation's efforts and reiterated the need to better define what college students need to learn in order to participate and succeed in today's world.

The book *Academically Adrift: Limited Learning on College Campuses* (Arum & Roksa, 2011) presented the results of research conducted at twenty-four colleges and universities in the United States. More than 2,300 undergraduate students were surveyed to find an answer to the question "What if sending students to college did not necessarily ensure that much was learned once there?" The authors reported that "gains in student performance are disturbingly low; a pattern of limited learning is prevalent on contemporary college campuses" (p. 30). The authors found little evidence that students gain much in critical thinking, complex reasoning, and writing skills during their time in college. Given the book's conclusions, the headlines in the popular press were not surprising: "Study Shows College Students Not Learning Enough"; "Report: College Students Not Learning Much"; "Student Tracking Finds Limited Learning in College." With the escalating expenses of tuition and a still difficult national economy, one might ask, if students don't learn enough while they are in college, how much sense does it make for them to go in the first place? Why should someone incur the expense and take on the significant debt often required to finance a higher education if not enough learning is occurring?

During his State of the Union address, President Obama stated, "Of course, the education race doesn't end with a high school diploma. To compete, higher education must be within the reach of every American" (2011). To do this, the president asked the Congress to make permanent a $10,000 tuition-tax credit for four years of college so that "America will once again have the highest proportion of college graduates in the world." The stated national goal of enrolling more students in college and providing much-needed financial assistance to pay for their degrees of course presents a golden opportunity for admission officers and enrollment managers. The financial challenges for some students may be eased with tuition tax credits being made permanent. Yet with the findings reported by Arum and Roksa (2011), the question "What will be learned?" remains.

Perhaps part of the answer can be found in the Lumina Foundation's document *The Degree Qualifications Profile* (2011). The profile "illustrates clearly what students should be expected to know and be able to do once they earn their degrees" (p. 1) whether at the associate, bachelor's or master's level. Beyond proposing a "set of reference points that benchmark what it should take for students to earn a degree at each of the three levels addressed—in addition to whatever an institution requires in terms of credits, grades and specific course completion" (p. 2), the profile serves as a resource to encourage colleges and universities to develop or further enhance their assessment efforts. With the profile as a guide, students and their families can ask, or even demand, what learning can be expected while enrolled at their institution of choice and how they will know it has been attained.

The American Association of Colleges and Universities (AAC&U) is a recognized national leader in advocating the advancement and improvement of a liberal education for all students. It advocates four key strategies for raising student achievement: "clear description of the knowledge, skills, responsibilities, and applied learning" that college graduates need; the kinds of teaching and learning strategies that place the student at the "center of educational focus and assessment"; approaches that challenge students to do their best work and not rely "only on grades and the number of credit hours earned as the basis for their college degrees"; and a commitment to achieving a "liberating and empowering education" (AAC&U, 2011, p. 4). In its statement of support for the Lumina Foundation's degree profile, AAC&U states that it "represents a much-needed commitment to set and achieve greater expectations for all learners, whatever their background or pathway to and through college" (2011, p. 5). Reports like this put increasing pressure on colleges and universities to ensure that their students acquire the necessary competencies to be successful in their careers and become contributing members of society as a result of earning their college degrees. It also pressures institutions to provide clear and compelling data that demonstrates that this is the case.

The focus of many higher educational institutions is mostly on the financial concerns of students and their families. One way of addressing these concerns is to shorten the time it takes to earn an undergraduate degree and therefore cut the price of higher education. As shown in this book, depending on the model chosen, a shorter time does not necessarily cut the delivery costs for institutions and in fact may increase those costs relative to income and hasten some institutions' demise. With the questions raised by the research of Arum and Roksa (2011) and the need to ensure that college graduates are learning what they need to, simply accelerating the pace of a college education is insufficient and likely counterproductive unless other measures are taken.

Although there is no silver bullet or only one way to address the current challenges facing higher education, the Integrated Three-Year-Degree Model is one option that has been proven to work. Not only does this model control and even reduce prices and costs, but the competency-based curriculum is more responsive to the needs of society and business without sacrificing educational quality. In addition, it allows institutions to more effectively compete for and retain students. In this era of financial uncertainty and pressures to address the criticism about how well prepared college graduates are, there could be a high potential for the adoption of an integrated three-year model. The top 10–20 percent of four-year-degree-granting institutions will likely remain fairly insulated from the need to change much structurally, at least for the time being. However, that will not be the case for many other public and private nonprofit colleges and universities. The first adopters of the Integrated, Competency-Based Three-Year Model will likely be small, mostly private colleges and universities, because they represent the largest segment of institutions across the United States. These institutions, especially the tuition-driven ones, will see this option as an opportunity to attract additional enrollments by being more responsive to society's concerns about rising tuition prices and concerns about the readiness of graduates to enter the workforce and society.

Public institutions that consider changing to the integrated, competency-based three-year approach will likely do so as a result of state legislative action as has recently been seen in Rhode Island (State of Rhode Island, 2009) and in Florida. Large public and private universities may also choose to make a three-year-degree model available to their students, although this segment may be decidedly slower to adopt and implement this option due to their size. One example is the University of California system, which has laid the groundwork for the introduction of an accelerated model (University of California, 2010).

It is evident that unless fundamental changes occur soon, a college education may be financially out of reach for more and more of our citizens (Fischer, 2011). And even if the financial challenges are somehow resolved, students earning degrees without developing the knowledge, skills, and competencies needed to succeed in the workplace and to become contributing members of society will have profound consequences. The consequences will impact our nation's ability to compete in a global marketplace and will, ultimately, impede the advancement of knowledge.

The Three-Year University: Design Principles

It is one thing to create an integrated three-year degree at the program level. It is quite another thing to create it at the school or university level. Imagine what an integrated three-year school of business or an integrated three-year school of arts and sciences would look like. Although they may not be hard to imagine, what may be daunting is how to get there. Although this book does not pretend to have all the answers, it can at least outline some of the challenges.

The Framework

All three of the three-year-degree models reviewed for this book are committed to the attainment of 120 credit hours along with the associated knowledge and skills. Students receive standard transcripts. Some universities will want to try out a single integrated three-year program to see if it can work well within the existing four-year framework. Others will want to convert one or more existing four-year programs to three years. Some institutions may want to wait and watch, and there will be those that choose to do nothing.

The transformation of many existing four-year institutions into ones that deliver only integrated three-year programs could take some time. It is likely that the benefits of three-year programs will become so obvious that enormous pressure will be exerted by students and their parents, by trustees, and by legislative bodies. The tipping point may come when enough four-year students in institutions offering both three- and four-year options perceive it to be unfair that they must pay four years of tuition while their three-year counterparts are only charged for three.

Three-year schools within universities or entire universities can be places where cross-disciplinary collaboration in the service of an integrated curriculum is the norm for faculty and where close articulation with employers about student competencies is the standard operating procedure. This would result in a situation where students appreciate a well-organized and efficiently delivered curriculum that allows them to avoid the expense of an extra year of tuition.

At the very least the conversation about three-year programs and curriculum reform needs to become a wider national discussion so that others can join the conversation about how students' higher education experience can be reshaped in order to improve efficiencies while enhancing quality. This wider goal represents a movement of higher education toward a more sustainable price and cost structure that at the same time ensures a more competitive environment for nonprofit institutions.

Institutional leaders interested in pursuing the development of a three-year-degree school or university will want to consider the key design principles that need to be developed in order to ensure the long-term sustainability of the curriculum. These six design principles include a competency-based curriculum, curriculum integration, a student-centered learning culture, intensive use of technology, cohort- and team-intensive class environments, and scalability.

Competency-Based Curriculum

Developing a set of competencies that matches the institutional mission can contribute to the creation of a powerful academic experience for the learner, especially when delivered in an active teaching and learning environment. The competencies define the desired outcomes for the program, school, or university and require that faculty reconsider curriculum content and sequencing in order to assure that it will result in the learner's achievement of the competencies. This type of alignment is the hallmark of modern curriculum reform.

As this book points out, institutions and professional associations are calling for a move away from the credit hour/seat-time measure that has dogged higher education for the last one hundred years. A recent Association of American Colleges and Universities publication (2011) stated that "the credit-hour approach is seriously out of touch with society's current need for graduates who can adapt and expand existing knowledge and skills to meet new challenges and unscripted problems in every sphere of life" (p. 5). An internal memo to a college faculty by Schiffman promotes competency-based curriculum that by design "focuses on the student as a learning, developing individual. In contrast to a course-based curriculum, it values the global effectiveness of the student's development above the local efficiency of the subject matter delivery" (as quoted in Evers, Rush, & Berdrow, 1998, p. 208). A competency-designed-curriculum approach elevates the discussion from a subject matter debate to a more holistic conversation regarding the development of the student as a learner and participant in the learning process.

How much of a challenge is this? It is a significant challenge but one worth doing whether or not a three-year model is contemplated. Chapter 4 provides some perspective on how to approach these challenges.

Curriculum Integration

Like a master gardener who intentionally designs a garden to bloom with vivid colors throughout the summer, faculty can purposefully design curricula so that students are challenged on an ongoing basis to expand their knowledge and skills and gain deeper awareness and understanding of the human condition. Faculty are subject matter experts. However, they must also be capable of designing course content that supports and assists in achieving the broader outcomes for the relevant major and the overall program-level competencies embedded in the curriculum. This latter skill set is relatively new for faculty, because for years their focus was solely on courses within their discipline.

As the academy begins to shift away from the notion of seat time, a highly integrated curriculum will become an imperative for campus leaders. Accomplishing this aim will necessitate that faculty from all disciplines collaborate in the design and execution of a holistic and purposeful curriculum, a curriculum that will prepare graduates to successfully compete in the twenty-first century.

This design principle of the three-year university requires university leadership with the vision, courage, and skills to mobilize the faculty and provide the resources necessary for success.

Student-Centered Learning Culture

As reported by Tagg (2003) and Diamond (2008), there is an increasing shift toward a more student-centered learning experience with the faculty member transitioning from a traditional lecture format to a student-centered learning paradigm. This approach requires the faculty member to use a variety of techniques to facilitate student learning, an approach that also promotes a more active learning experience. A few examples of these methods include the use of case studies, computer-based simulations, team projects, and debates on complex theories and concepts. In each instance the faculty member is the facilitator of student learning rather than the director of student learning. The student-centered classroom is an important feature in the transition to an integrated three-year-degree program, school, or university. This approach together with a competency-based curriculum has a good chance of improving student learning outcomes.

This design principle requires faculty buy-in and academic leadership from the top levels of the institution's administration within the constraints of faculty academic pedagogical freedom. This can be a challenge and will take the insights and leadership abilities of top administrators to set the direction for such an endeavor.

Intensive Use of Technology

Colleges and universities will continue to become more technologically sophisticated over the next five years. It is likely that what began at many universities as distinct and separate programmatic areas or divisions of online learning will begin to merge back into the center of the academic house. This shift will be driven by full-time students' demand for access to online, hybrid, and blended courses. Consider the *Chronicle of Higher Education*'s special issue on online learning (November 5, 2010), where it was reported that over half of the University of Central Florida's 56,000 students completed at least one hybrid or blended class. During that same academic year an additional 2,700 students completed classes in three different modes of learning. The artificial barriers erected in order to allow the online programs to grow separately from the traditional academic departments are ready to be removed. Bringing the online delivery mode back into the central academic fold will ensure that the different types of learning approaches can be effectively used to meet the needs of full-time learners and in particular those students in a three-year program.

As Zemke, Raines, and Filipczak (2000) point out in *Generations at Work*, the Nexters generation, born between 1980 and 2000, that now populates college and university classrooms has grown up digitally. As a result these students think about and use technology in ways that make some faculty uncomfortable. One challenge will be to help faculty make the transition to becoming facilitators in learning communities where students' course content is completely stored on their e-book readers, handheld devices, or in the Internet cloud.

How big a challenge is this for institutions? It depends on where they stand now with respect to the use of learning technologies. Once again, administrative leadership and vision along with faculty buy-in are crucial components for success.

Cohort- and Team-Intensive Class Environments

In designing a three-year university, cohort grouping and team-intensive experiences must be given prominent consideration. The term *cohort* is used here to denote a set of students that move together through various learning experiences (that is, modules). The term *team* denotes a group of students organized within a cohort. Grouping students in a learning-community cohort or ad hoc teams offers several benefits from a learning-centered perspective. First, students can establish an identity much more rapidly within a cohort or team. Second, cohorts and teams themselves can establish a sense of identity as a group. Third, students establish natural support networks that advance the needs of the participants. Trust-based relationships can develop, leading to systems of mutual support and accountability (Katzenbach & Smith, 1993). Other benefits of teams include the opportunity to make better decisions and the opportunity for improved creativity.

Student teams can be remixed in different modules so that students experience different dynamics within a cohort from module to module. With the start of a new semester or term, new cohorts can be configured, thus creating new dynamics for the students. Finally the widespread use of teams across the curriculum develops and reinforces a competency related to teamwork and leadership.

What are the challenges involved in this principle? They are many and they somewhat depend upon scale. In small universities, putting together cohorts may be rather straightforward and easy to do. For larger institutions, creating cohorts may present a challenge of a high order. And this is where technology can play a significant role. Today's students are already members of many informal cohorts and teams via their participation in social networks. Extending and formalizing that paradigm to the three-year university may help mitigate the barriers to creating cohorts and teams at large institutions.

Scalability

Scalability is last on the list not because it is less important than the other principles but because it is the most important one in some respects. Implementing a new curriculum can be a challenging task. However, designing and implementing a three-year-degree curriculum for an entire university or school using the principles outlined here will surely require altering past administrative thinking and practices.

Scalability is the ability to create a curriculum model that can serve large numbers of students and involve a large number of faculty members. It is the ability to build on prior learning sequencing, and it is flexible enough to account for the ebb and flow of students into and out of the curriculum. In order to deliver an integrated competency-based program in six semesters, modules may need to be delivered in some alternative formats. For example, the best method for laying the foundation for a Problem Solving competency may be for students to have more time-intensive learning experiences (for example, seven weeks of more frequent meetings). Conversely, when it comes to an Ethics and Social Responsibility competency, teaching faculty may agree that a longer timeframe may lead to better results (for example, longer than fifteen weeks).

The key is to ensure that the needs of the learner drive the design and delivery of the content rather than the perceived needs of the administrative unit. Striking a balance between the design and delivery of a functional curriculum while making sure that the curriculum is scalable will be of the utmost importance in assuring faculty and institutional adoption.

The three-year university design will need to adhere to all levels of accreditation standards and may need to include options for students who wish to complete their program in four rather than three years. Varsity athletes may be one example of such students. Another example may be students who just feel that they need a fourth year to fully master the competencies and to mature socially. The university will also need to provide reasonable mechanisms for students to transfer into and out of programs without significant loss of credit.

Is scalability a challenge? Yes—a big one. Will it take the courage, imagination, and vision of top-level administrators to consider changing some of their traditional practices? Certainly it will. This book offers no magic bullets but it does hope to generate a conversation where the synergy produced by many contributors will create imaginative solutions.

Now, Not Later

There is a sense of urgency in the air. Is there a magic bullet to save higher education from the perfect storm of price and cost spirals that threaten the survival of many institutions and complaints from some about how much students actually learn? Probably not. But, this book shows that an integrated three-year model may have as good a chance as any. Maybe even a better chance.

Is a three-year school or university doable? Why not? Imagine having the opportunity to design, build, and open a brand new university as has been done around the world in recent years. Imagine that you can design this university from the ground up based on the Integrated Three-Year Model. Such a university is not hard to imagine. From that thought, think about how your existing four-year institution can transition a program or programs using the Integrated Three-Year Model. Then, think about how it can transition to a completely integrated three-year school or an entire university. Things get more complicated.

But if such a transition can save your education institution from closing, then perhaps solving such a complicated problem is worth the effort. After all, a three-year university has a good likelihood of attracting students who previously might not have enrolled and of being able to retain them. A successful transition to an integrated three-year model will very much depend upon your institution's agility and leadership. We hope this book will stimulate the kind of thinking that contributes to the ongoing conversation.

Appendix A

Colleges and Universities Offering
Three-Year-Degree Programs

| | | Prior | | |
Institution	State	Learning	Integrated	Accelerated
Arcadia University	PA			X
Atlanta Christian College	GA			X
Baldwin-Wallace College	OH			X
Ball State University	IN			X
Bates College	ME			X
Bethany College	WV			X
Caldwell College	NJ			X
Chatham University	PA			X
Endicott College	MA			X
Ferris State University	MI			X
Florida State University	FL	X		X
Franklin and Marshall College	PA			X
Georgia Perimeter College	GA			X
Grace College and Seminary	IN			X
Green Mountain College	VT			X
Hartwick College	NY			X
Judson College	AL			X
Lake Forest College	IL			X
Lipscomb University	TN			X
Lynn University	FL			X
Manchester College	IN			X
Mount Olive College	NC			X

Institution	State	Prior Learning	Integrated	Accelerated
Northern Arizona University Yavapai Campus	AZ			X
Regis College	MA			X
Russell Sage College	NY			X
Southern New Hampshire University	NH		X	
Southern Oregon University	OR	X		X
St. John's University	NY			X
UMass Amherst	MA	X		X
University of Charleston–W. Virginia	WV	X	X	
University of Houston–Victoria	TX			X
University of Maine at Fort Kent	ME	X		X
University of New Haven	CT			X
University of North Carolina–Greensboro	NC	X		X
University of South Dakota	SD			X
University of Southern Florida	FL	X		X
University of Virginia	VA			
University of Washington	WA			X
University of Wisconsin Superior	WI			X
Ursuline College	OH			X
Valparaiso University	IN			X
Western Illinois and Eastern Iowa Community College District	IL and IA			X
Western Illinois University	IL			X

Note: Information current as of June 2011.

Appendix B

National Graduation and Retention Statistics

Chapter 2 reported that the national graduation rate in six years for private colleges was 45.2 percent and for public colleges, 45.1 percent—for traditional selectivity (ACT, 2010a). ACT (2010a) defines traditional selectivity as "majority admitted from top 50 percent of H.S. class." Chapter 5 reported that the national average graduation rate in four years was 39.2 percent for private institutions offering bachelor's and master's degrees only with traditional selectivity. Also reported was that the national average graduation rates in five years and six years were 50.4 percent and 52.1 percent, respectively, for the same types of institutions (ACT, 2010c).

Chapter 5 reported that in 2008, the U.S. national first- to second-year retention rate for four-year-degree students in private institutions offering bachelor's and master's degrees only with traditional selectivity was 70.5 percent (ACT, 2010b).

The reason ACT statistics were used rather than statistics from the National Center for Education Statistics (NCES, 2010b, 2010c) or the NCHEMS Information Center for Higher Education Policymaking and Analysis (NCHEMS, 2010a, 2010b) is that the ACT data includes institutional selectivity. Southern New Hampshire University's Three-Year-Degree Program selectivity is traditional. Private-college statistics were reported because

Southern New Hampshire University is a private, nonprofit institution.

Even if NCES or NCHEMS data had been used, the comparison results between the Southern New Hampshire University graduation rates and first- to second-year retention rates would still be quite favorable to the Integrated Three-Year Program.

Appendix C

Academic Plan for Three-Year Communications Module

Academic Plan Cover Sheet

Three-Year Bachelor of Science in Business Administration

Module: Communications Module

Modular Sub-Component: Eng 120, College Composition I, Communications Foundation

Program Year: Year One, First Semester, Weeks 1–5

1. Intra Modular Sub-Component Linking Themes:
    a. Student as problem solver
    b. Student as environment builder
    c. Student as effective group/team member
    d. Student as influencer and motivator

2. Intra Modular Linking Themes:
    a. Student as effective manager and leader
    b. Student as effective manager of human resources
    c. Student as strategic thinker and analyst

3. Inter Modular Linking Themes for the Year:
    a. Student as manager and leader

4. Other Modular Sub-Components:
    a. Writing, Research and Presentation

5. Concurrently Running MSCs:

    a.   Foundations of Computer Information Technology (CIT)
F = Items marked "F" refer to knowledge and skills which
are foundational to the students in the module as indicated.
R = Items marked "R" refer to knowledge and skills which
are reinforcing to the students in the module as indicated.
C = Activity contributes to the students' awareness of
certain knowledge and skills prior to their foundational
experience.

Modular Sub-Component Academic Plan

Modular Sub-Component: **Communications Foundation**
Program Year: **Year One, Semester One, Weeks 1–4.4**

1. STRATEGY: To develop and lay the foundation of communication skills and knowledge required of professionals today.

2. GOALS: COMMUNICATION-COMPETENCY #1

    a.   To master written communication that is appropriate for
an entry-level management position and for advancement
thereafter.

    b.   To master verbal (oral) communication that is appropriate
for an entry-level management position and for advancement thereafter.

    c.   To master electronic communication that is appropriate for
an entry-level management position and for advancement
thereafter.

2. IMPLEMENTING   ACTIVITIES: COMMUNICATION-
COMPETENCY #1

    a.   To have students produce a word processed, grammatically
correct essay and series of essay drafts leading to a finished
product.

> C1-F This implementing activity is a foundational activity for Competency #1 (Communication)

b. To have students give an oral presentation that is carefully organized and adapted in style and content to its audience.

> C1-F This implementing activity is a foundational activity for Competency #1 (Communication)

c. To have students work effectively in groups to draft and edit each other's work.

> C1-F This implementing activity is a foundational activity for Competency #1 (Communication)

> C6-C This implementing activity is a contributing activity for Competency #6 (Group Membership)

> C9-C This implementing activity is a contributing activity for Competency #9 (Interpersonal Skills)

d. To have students participate in small group discussions, workshops and instructor conferences throughout the drafting process in order to give students feedback on written papers and interpersonal skills.

> C1-F This implementing activity is a foundational activity for Competency #1 (Communication)

> C5-C This implementing activity is a contributing activity for Competency #5 (Organizational Leadership)

> C9-C This implementing activity is a contributing activity for Competency #9 (Interpersonal Skills)

e. To have students complete and discuss readings in memoir models, the writing process and editing techniques (standards and expectations).

> C1-F This implementing activity is a foundational activity for Competency #1 (Communication)

f. To have students complete readings and videotape exercises on the fundamentals of effective public speaking (preparation to present memoir essay orally using manuscript method).

> C1-F This implementing activity is a foundational activity for Competency #1 (Communication)

g. To have students give an oral presentation of memoir essay using effective presentation techniques, by way of self-introduction.

> C1-F This implementing activity is a foundational activity for Competency #1 (Communication)

h. To have students keep a learning journal (study guides for modular credit) on all readings and video presentations.

> C1-F This implementing activity is a foundational activity for Competency #1 (Communication)

i. Students working in small groups throughout the first communications module will work weekly on asynchronous and synchronous communications projects.

> C2-R This implementing activity is a reinforcement activity for Competency #2 (Computer and Information Technology)

> C6-C This implementing activity is a contributing activity for Competency #6 (Group Membership)

> C9-C This implementing activity is a contributing activity for Competency #9 (Interpersonal Skills)

j. Students will be required to use online techniques at least one day per week for the purposes of one-on-one and group communication.

> C2-R This implementing activity is a reinforcement activity for Competency #2 (Computer and Information Technology)

k. Students will complete at least four assignments (including drafts as one assignment) which will be written utilizing Microsoft Word.

   C2-R This implementing activity is a reinforcement activity for Competency #2 (Computer and Information Technology)

l. To have students participate in five or more group assignments that will demand group collaborative work and require peer assessment.

   C6-C This implementing activity is a contributing activity for Competency #6 (Group Membership)

   C9-C This implementing activity is a contributing activity for Competency #9 (Interpersonal Skills)

m. To require students to critique (both written and oral) at least four peer projects over the course of this module.

   C9-C This implementing activity is a contributing activity for Competency #9 (Interpersonal Skills)

Appendix D

Academic Plan for Three-Year Management Module

Academic Plan Cover Sheet

Three-Year Bachelor of Science in Business Administration

Module: Management Module
Modular Sub-Component: OL 125, Manager Skills Foundation
Program Year: Year One, First Semester

1. Intra Modular Sub-Component (Single Module) Linking Themes:
   a. Student as problem solver
   b. Student as effective communicator
   c. Student as effective group/team leader
   d. Student as effective group/team member
   e. Student as influencer and motivator
2. Intra Modular (Two or More Modules in the Same Academic Year) Linking Themes:
   a. Student as effective manager and leader
   b. Student as effective manager of human resources
   c. Student as strategic thinker and analyst

3. Inter Modular Linking Themes for the Year:

   a.   Student as manager and leader

   b.   Humanities and the individual

4. Other Modular Sub-Components:

   a.   OL 215, Principles of Management

       F = Items marked "F" refer to knowledge and skills which are foundational to the students in the module as indicated.

       R = Items marked "R" refer to knowledge and skills which are reinforcing to the students in the module as indicated.

       C = Items marked "C" refer to knowledge and skills which are contributed to the students in the module as indicated.

Modular Sub-Component Academic Plan

Modular Sub-Component: **OL 125 Manager Skills Foundation**
Program Year: **Year One, Semester One**

1. STRATEGY: To develop the basic interactive skills of the manager by laying foundations in: (1) Interpersonal skills, (2) Analytical and creative problem-solving, (3) Organizational leadership, and (4) Group membership by involving the student in both theoretical and applied exercises.

2. Goals: Communication—Competency #1

   a.   To understand the role of perception, communication, motivation, leadership and group dynamics in human interaction.

   b.   To understand why effective interaction leads to personal, social, business and career success.

c. To understand that successful interaction and mutual influence lead to personal, social and career growth.

d. To understand the importance of interpersonal skills in managing and leading a diverse work force where diversity includes gender, race, religion, ethnicity, nationality and socioeconomic class.

2. Implementing Activities: Communication—Competency #1

a. Participate in a series of self-evaluations designed to increase the student's level of self-awareness and interpersonal strength.

C1-F This implementing activity is a foundational activity for Competency #1 (Communication)

b. Participate in a series of small-group communications exercises designed to heighten student awareness of the communications process and its importance in the influence and information transmission process.

C1-F This implementing activity is a foundational activity for Competency #1 (Communication)

C3-F This implementing activity is a foundational activity for Competency #3 (Problem Solving)

C4-R This implementing activity is a reinforcement activity for Competency #4 (Teamwork)

c. Participate in a series of small-group evaluations and exercises that are designed to equip students to relate to members of a diverse work force.

C1-F This implementing activity is a foundational activity for Competency #1 (Communication)

C3-F This implementing activity is a foundational activity for Competency #3 (Problem Solving)

C4-R This implementing activity is a reinforcement activity for Competency #4 (Teamwork)

    d. Observe and critique the interpersonal behaviors of four peers who functioned as members of an intact work group in the problem solving process.

        C1-R This implementing activity is a reinforcement activity for Competency #1 (Communication)

        C1-F This implementing activity is a foundational activity for Competency #1 (Communication)

        C3-R This implementing activity is a reinforcement activity for Competency #3 (Problem Solving)

        C4-R This implementing activity is a reinforcement activity for Competency #4 (Teamwork)

    e. In written form, summarize the results of an interview of a faculty, staff or administrator focused on how the interviewee addresses any one of the four key competencies central to this management module.

        C1-R This implementing activity is a reinforcement activity for Competency #1 (Communication)

        C1-F This implementing activity is a foundational activity for Competency #1 (Communication)

3. Goals: Problem Solving—Competency #3

    a. To understand the role of problem detection and problem solving in personal, social and management decision making.

    b. To understand the role and necessity of creativity in problem solving.

    c. To understand and apply a logical, analytical process when problem solving and be able to modify this process to suit the situation.

    d. To understand the various techniques that can be used to facilitate the problem solving process.

    e. To understand the various problem-solving styles that can be used under different circumstances and to understand the circumstances under which a change of style is necessary.

   f. To understand how to analyze the nature of a problem situation.

   g. To understand how to evaluate alternative courses of action.

   h. To understand that old solutions do not always fit new problems.

3. Implementing Activities: Problem Solving—Competency #3

   a. As a member of an intact work group participate in brainstorming, nominal grouping, multi-voting and affinity diagramming exercises.

        C1-R This implementing activity is a reinforcement activity for Competency #1 (Communication)

        C3-F This implementing activity is a foundational activity for Competency #3 (Problem Solving)

        C4-R This implementing activity is a reinforcement activity for Competency #4 (Teamwork)

   b. Using the problem-solving process, participate both individually and as a member of a work group in the detection, analysis and solution of a series of human relations problems.

        C1-R This implementing activity is a reinforcement activity for Competency #1 (Communication)

        C3-F This implementing activity is a foundational activity for Competency #3 (Problem Solving)

        C4-R This implementing activity is a reinforcement activity for Competency #4 (Teamwork)

4. Goals: Leadership—Competency #10

   a. To understand the dynamics of leadership as an interpersonal and intra-organizational process.

    b. To understand and apply group leadership skills.

    c. To understand and apply transformational and situational leadership techniques.

    d. To understand how to lead a group in the problem-solving process.

4. Implementing Activities: Leadership—Competency #10

    a. Function as the leader in an intact work group solving human relations problems.

> C1-R This implementing activity is a reinforcement activity for Competency #9 (Communication)
>
> C3-R This implementing activity is a reinforcement activity for Competency #3 (Problem Solving)
>
> C4-R This implementing activity is a reinforcement activity for Competency #4 (Teamwork)
>
> C10-F This implementing activity is a foundational activity for Competency #10 (Leadership)

    b. Observe and critique the interpersonal behaviors of peers who were work group leaders.

> C1-R This implementing activity is a reinforcement activity for Competency #1 (Communication)
>
> C3-R This implementing activity is a reinforcement activity for Competency #3 (Problem Solving)
>
> C4-R This implementing activity is a reinforcement activity for Competency #4 (Teamwork)
>
> C10-F This implementing activity is a foundational activity for Competency #10 (Leadership)

    c. Conduct a 10 minute briefing, using computer graphics, where the student must explain an aspect of the leadership process.

> C1-R This implementing activity is a reinforcement activity for Competency #1 (Communication)

C2-R This implementing activity is a reinforcement activity for Competency #2 (Information Technology)

C10-F This implementing activity is a foundational activity for Competency #10 (Leadership)

d. While acting as leader, analyze a leadership situation and use the appropriate leadership style, conflict management style, problem solving style and communications style.

C1-R This implementing activity is a reinforcement activity for Competency #1 (Communication)

C3-R This implementing activity is a reinforcement activity for Competency #3 (Problem Solving)

C10-F This implementing activity is a foundational activity for Competency #10 (Leadership)

e. Participate individually and as a member of a group in an in-class exercise applying the situational leadership model to a number of scenarios.

C3-R This implementing activity is a reinforcement activity for Competency #3 (Problem Solving)

C4-F This implementing activity is a foundational activity for Competency #4 (Teamwork)

C10-F This implementing activity is a foundational activity for Competency #10 (Leadership)

f. Prepare and discuss a one-page statement for your philosophy of leadership.

C1-R This implementing activity is a reinforcement activity for Competency #1 (Communication)

C10-F This implementing activity is a foundational activity for Competency #10 (Leadership)

5. Goals: Teamwork—Competency #4

a. To understand small group dynamics.

b. Participate as an effective group member in structured and unstructured situations.

    c. Understand group problem-solving techniques.

    d. Understand how to encourage other group members to participate in the process.

    e. Understand the basics of team building.

    f. Understand the process and dynamics by which group member behavior creates synergy.

5. Implementing Activities: Teamwork—Competency #4

    a. In four work group situations involving human relations problems, function as an effective, contributing group member.

> C1-R This implementing activity is a reinforcement activity for Competency #1 (Communication)
>
> C3-R This implementing activity is a reinforcement activity for Competency #3 (Problem Solving)
>
> C4-F This implementing activity is a foundational activity for Competency #4 (Teamwork)

    b. Monitor, evaluate and critique group member behavior in four situations when human relations problems are analyzed.

> C1-R This implementing activity is a reinforcement activity for Competency #1 (Communication)
>
> C3-R This implementing activity is a reinforcement activity for Competency #3 (Problem Solving)
>
> C4-F This implementing activity is a foundational activity for Competency #4 (Teamwork)

    c. Participate in several group exercises where group dynamics lead to synergy.

> C1-R This implementing activity is a reinforcement activity for Competency #1 (Communication)
>
> C3-R This implementing activity is a reinforcement activity for Competency #3 (Problem Solving)

       C4-F This implementing activity is a foundational activity for Competency #4 (Teamwork)

d. As a member of a group, research, prepare and deliver an in-class presentation not to exceed 15 minutes on a topic selected by the group and approved by the instructor.

       C1-R This implementing activity is a reinforcement activity for Competency #1 (Communication)

       C4-F This implementing activity is a foundational activity for Competency #4 (Teamwork)

       C8-F This implementing activity is a foundational activity for Competency #3 (Research)

Appendix E

Model Syllabus for Three-Year Human Relations Module

Model Module Syllabus

School of Business

OL 125 Human Relations in Administration (3-Yr)

Manchester Day—Three-Year Degree Program

Faculty Name:

Office Location:

Email Address:

Office Phone:

Office Hours:

Blackboard Workspace Address: http://blackboard.com

Required TEXTBOOK(s) and Supplemental Materials

Use current adopted text(s).

Supplementary readings, cases, inventories and handouts as supplied by the instructor.

———————

Module Prerequisites: None

Module Description: Four cardinal managerial competencies are introduced and developed as a result of student involvement in this first sub-component of management module one: interpersonal skills, problem solving, group membership, and organizational leadership. Through the use of readings, cases, class challenge initiatives, group and individual work, and presentations, students will acquire knowledge and develop the human relation skills essential for current and future managerial success. Participation in this module will result in each student significantly increasing his/her personal level of effectiveness.

Topics for Discussion: Class discussions and related learning tools and strategies will focus on: perception and personality; attitudes, self-concept, values and ethics; communication; conflict; trust; motivation; ethical power and politics; team dynamics and leadership; creative problem solving and decision making; organizational change and culture and global diversity.

Module Sub-Component Key Competencies:

Competency #4	Problem Solving
Competency #5	Organizational Leadership
Competency #6	Group Membership
Competency #9	Interpersonal Skills

Competency #4

"To conduct analytical and creative problem detection and problem solving."

Knowledge and skill mastery is commensurate with the needs of an entry-level management position in a Fortune 500 company.

(Three-Year-Degree Program Strategic Plan, Jan. 1997)

Foundational Goals for Competency #4

a. To understand the role of problem detection and problem solving in personal, social, and management decision-making.

b. To understand the role and necessity of creativity in problem solving.

c. To understand and apply a logical, analytical process when problem solving and be able to modify this process to suit the situation.

d. To understand the various techniques that can be used to facilitate the problem solving process.

e. To understand the various problem-solving styles that can be used under different circumstances and to understand the circumstances under which you would change your style.

f. To understand how to analyze the nature of a problem situation.

g. To understand how to evaluate alternative courses of action.

h. To understand that old solutions do not fit new problems.

Competency #5

"To understand how and be able to function as an effective team, group, and organizational leader."

Knowledge and skill mastery is commensurate with the needs of an entry-level management position in a Fortune 500 company.

(*Three-Year-Degree Program Strategic Plan*, Jan. 1997)

Foundational Goals for Competency #5

a. To understand the dynamics of leadership as an interpersonal and intra-organizational process.

b. To understand and apply group leadership skills.

c. To understand and apply transformational and situational leadership techniques.

d. To understand how to lead a group in the problem-solving process.

Competency #6

"To understand how and be able to function as an effective group and/or team member."

Knowledge and skill mastery is commensurate with the needs of an entry-level management position in a Fortune 500 company.

(*Three-Year-Degree Program Strategic Plan*, Jan. 1997)

Foundational Goals for Competency #6

a. To understand small group dynamics.

b. Participate as an effective group member in structured and unstructured situations.

c. Understand group problem solving techniques.

d. Understand how to encourage other group members to participate in the process.

e. Understand the basics of team building.

Competency #9

"To develop a broad range of interpersonal skills to use in multicultural and diverse work force settings."

Knowledge and skill mastery is commensurate with the needs of an entry-level management position in a Fortune 500 company.

(*Three-Year-Degree Program Strategic Plan*, Jan. 1997)

Foundational Goals for Competency #9

a. To understand the role of perception, communication, motivation, leadership and group dynamics in human interaction.

b. To understand why effective interaction leads to personal, social, business, and career success.

c. To understand that successful interaction and mutual influence lead to personal, social, and career growth.

d. To understand the importance of interpersonal skills in managing and leading a diverse work force, where diversity includes gender, race, religion, ethnicity, nationality, and socioeconomic class.

Outcomes: The following outcomes will be achieved at the conclusion of the sub-component of Management Module One.

1. Define important concepts in human relations, including trends and challenges such as deregulations, litigation, a service economy, a global economy, an aging work force, growing work force diversity, changing educational levels and goals, changing values and expectations, and technology.

2. Understand that personality is a relatively stable set of traits that aid in explaining and predicting behavior.

3. To know that an attitude is a strong belief of feeling that an individual develops toward people and situations.

4. Discuss why power is a person's ability to influence another person's behavior; the seven bases of power are coercive, connection, reward, legitimate, referent, expert, and information.

5. Explain that motivation is the internal process leading to behavior to satisfy needs.

6. Understand that leadership is the process of influencing employees to work toward the achievement of a desired end.

7. Know that communications is the process of a sender transmitting a message to a receiver with mutual understanding, and where questioning, paraphrasing and effective feedback are important.

8. Know that one must be aware of communication barriers (perceptions, noise, emotion, filtering, trust and credibility, information overload, not listening, time and place, and media selection) and overcome them.

9. Understand that transactional analysis is a method of understanding behavior in interpersonal dynamics.

10. Define a group as two or more people interacting to achieve an objective, where there are functional, task, and informal groups, and where the two common committees used are ad hoc and standing committees.

11. Understand that the six components of group structure/dynamics include objectives, size, norms cohesiveness, status and roles.

12. To engage in a systematic process of problem detection and resolution.

Grading:

Midterm Exam	20%
Interview	20%
Team Presentation	20%
Final Exam	20%
Class Participation	20%

A student's grade is determined by the quality of his or her performance in the course. Grades are *earned* according to the following guidelines.

A = Outstanding   Work of distinctive quality not usually seen in other work. Shows superior grasp of course material and initiative on the part of the student. [A− = 90–92; A = 93–96; A+ 97–100]

B = Good   Work of above average or superior quality but less than outstanding. [B− = 80–82; B = 83–86; B+ = 87–89]

C = Average   Work of acceptable quality but without distinction. Meets stated requirements. [C− = 70–72; C = 73–76; C+ = 77–79]

D = Passing   Work of less than average quality but meets minimum requirements. [D = 60–64; D+ = 65–69]

F = Failing   Fails to meet minimum requirements.

Exams: There will be a mid-term and a final exam in the course. The exam format will include both short answer and essay questions. The purpose of these questions will be to offer students an opportunity to put into words what they know or understand a term, concept, or scenario to mean. It is important that students write clearly and thoughtfully so that the intended meaning is communicated in a way that is mutually understood.

Writing and Presentation Components:

Interview—20%

The purpose of this assignment is for you to interview a faculty, staff or administrator of your choice here at the college. The focus of this interview will be for you to learn how this person addresses any one of the four key competencies that are central in this module (see page 2 of the syllabus). The second part of this assignment will be for you to learn what this person perceives as "stress for them in the work place" and how they seek to deliberately manage these potential blocks to creativity. In your written document you are to provide the following:

I. Cover Page – To include your name, date, title

II. Background Summary of the Person Interviewed

   - Education background
   - Years in current position
   - Philosophy of work

III. List of Interview Questions Asked

IV. Summary of Interview – Here is where you will address the central themes of this assignment.

V. Optional – Your thoughts as a result of completing this project. Here is your opportunity to communicate any surprises or disappointments that you might have had as a result of completing this project.

Team Presentation—20%

From the subject headings listed below choose a topic that your team will investigate thoroughly over the next several weeks. While there are several outcomes for this project, the most significant single deliverable will be for your team to teach your classmates something new (add value) and significant about the topic. In addition to this requirement, teams will also be expected to do the following:

   - The project is to be team-driven; all members are expected to contribute to the project in meaningful ways. Work related and/or athletic responsibilities do not qualify as acceptable excuses for students to miss team meetings and/or to neglect other project responsibilities.

   - Your team is to find a minimum of two web sites that offer outstanding information regarding your topic and is to provide a one-page (double-spaced) assessment narrative as to the strengths of each web site (one page per web site).

- Your team, as part of the presentation and/or included in additional material provided to classmates, is to communicate how your presentation has attempted to add "new value" to your classmates.

- Presentations are to be 10–15 minutes in length.

- Team members will evaluate the performance of other team members. The grade for the project is team-based and, as such, member evaluations may result in the lowering of one or more team member grades.

Topics

Job satisfaction

Balanced scorecard

Values and norms

Strategic planning

Communication

Types of pay systems

Problem solving

TQM, process improvement

Benchmarking

Right brain/left brain for managers

ISO 9000

Knowledge management

ISO 14,000

Boundary management

Goal setting theory

Negotiating effectively

Teams wishing to investigate and present on a topic other than one of those noted above must submit their topic to the professor for approval.

Attendance: Attendance at all classes is essential since material not discussed in the text will be incorporated into weekly class meetings. A reduction in course grade may be given for more than two absences, and may result in withdrawal from the module.

Course Conduct and Standards:

- Active involvement in the learning process is expected.

- Come to class prepared, and participate in discussions.

- Take meaningful, useful notes.

- Students are responsible for all material presented and discussed in class, as well as related text material not covered in class.

- A good sense of humor is welcome at most any time.

- The final examination may be cumulative. The final exam will contain questions from previously tested areas where a skill or competency, such as indicated in the above module outcomes, are a significant factor.

- If you plan to be absent from a scheduled report or exam for a valid reason, please let me know in advance.

Appendix F

Flowchart of the Three-Year Bachelor of Science in Business Administration Development Activities

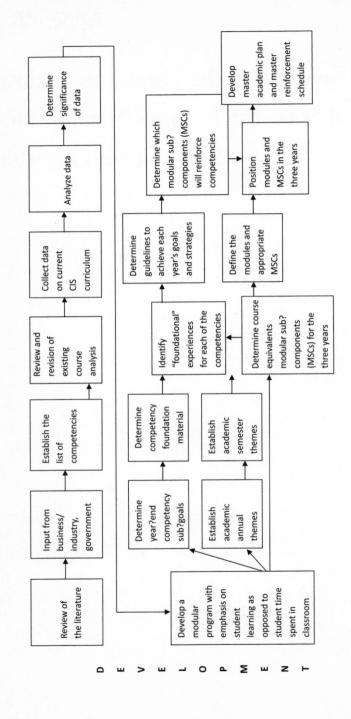

Appendix G

The SNHU Three-Year Program
Mission Statement

The Mission

The mission of the three-year baccalaureate program is to edu-
cate selected, qualified students who desire to major in Business
Administration/Business Leadership. The program is designed so
that students can:

a. *Succeed* in acquiring an entry-level position and advance in
their chosen professions and careers.

b. *Realize* individual potential and contribute to the betterment
of the local community and society at large.

c. *Be* effective leaders and proponents of change.

d. *Become* successful lifelong learners.

The university recognizes its obligation to deliver a high quality
program that prepares students for a profoundly changing business,
cultural, and geopolitical environment so they have the best chance
for personal and professional success and are equipped to provide
effective leadership. To achieve the mission students must work to
accomplish certain academic competencies. The university must
adopt the appropriate academic strategies and provide appropriate
resources to ensure the success of the program. The new paradigm
under which this program will operate thus recognizes the central

role of the student, the faculty, and college administrators to work jointly to accomplish the academic mission.

The University's Implementing Strategies and Supporting Plans

The university will ensure the success of the program and the achievement of its mission by pursuing multiple academic and administrative strategies which include:

a. Establishing a managed, competency-oriented, cross-curricular, interdisciplinary educational environment that is designed to build competencies in the student's major and in certain selected general education areas in a three-year period that equals or exceeds that which would occur in a traditional four-year program.

b. Integrating state-of-the-art computer and information technology into the learning process (see Computer Acquisition and Integration Plan).

c. Using diverse delivery systems for learning (see Delivery System Supporting Plan).

d. Requiring students to take responsibility for and actively participate in their own education (see Student Responsibility Supporting Plan).

e. Conducting an ongoing evaluation of the program and student progress toward competency achievement at the end of each year so competencies and/or the processes to achieve them are changed when needed and so the program achieves a condition of continuous evolution, change, and improvement (see Supporting Plan for Evaluation and Modification).

f. Implementing a learning-centered paradigm (see Learning Paradigm Supporting Plan).

g. Creating flexible, purposeful, integrated intra-disciplinary and interdisciplinary learning modules that are designed to accomplish certain competencies (see Cross-Curricular Competency Development Plan).

h. Employing faculty who are committed to the mission and the achievement of its attendant competencies and supporting strategies.

i. Adequately preparing and supporting faculty to function in the new paradigm (see Faculty Development Supporting Plan).

j. Admitting only those students to the program who manifest the psychological, social, and academic maturity and competence to succeed (see Student Recruitment and Admissions Plan).

k. In conjunction with paragraph j preceding, define the acceptance criteria that maximizes the possibility of success by the student and minimizes the chance of failure (see Student Recruitment and Admissions Plan).

l. Recording student achievement so students who transfer out of the program do so with three credit modules that have generally recognizable and accepted course names and grades (see Student Achievement Recording Plan).

m. Educating to lead a life of continual personal and professional learning.

n. Establishing and maintaining private sector business relationships, both profit and nonprofit, to provide contact and experiences for students to complement academic learning with work experience and enhance future employment opportunities (see Private Sector Support Plan).

o. Soliciting supplementary funding for the program for student scholarships, faculty support, and advanced computer information technology (see Supporting Plan for Grants).

References

AAC&U (Association of American Colleges and Universities). (2002). *Greater expectations: A new vision for learning as a nation goes to college*. Retrieved from http://www.greaterexpectations.org/

AAC&U. (2007). Essential learning outcomes. *College learning for the new global century: A report from the National Leadership Council for Liberal Education and America's Promise* (p. 12). Washington, DC: Association of American Colleges and Universities. Retrieved from http://www.uwyo.edu/accreditation/_files/docs /Essential_Learning_Outcomes.pdf

AAC&U. (2011). *AAC&U statement on the Lumina Foundation for Education's Proposed Degree Qualifications Profile*. Retrieved from http://www.aacu.org/about /statements/documents/lumina_dqs_2011.pdf

ACBSP (Association of Collegiate Business Schools and Programs). (2008). *ACBSP standards and criteria for demonstrating excellence in baccalaureate/graduate degree school and programs*. Overland Park, KS: Author.

ACT. (2010a). *National collegiate retention and persistence to degree rates*. Retrieved from http://www.act.org/research/policymakers/pdf/retain_2010.pdf

ACT. (2010b). *First- to second-year retention rates by four-year private institutions by institutional type and level of selectivity and degrees offered*. Retrieved from http:// www.act.org/research/policymakers/pdf/retain_2010.pdf

ACT. (2010c). *National persistence to degree rates by four-year private institutions by degrees offered and level of selectivity.* Retrieved from http://www.act.org/research /policymakers/pdf/retain_2010.pdf

Aldrich, C. (2009a). *Learning online with games, simulations, and virtual worlds: Strategies for online instruction.* San Francisco, CA: Jossey-Bass.

Aldrich, C. (2009b). *The complete guide to simulations and serious games: How the most valuable content will be created in the age beyond Gutenberg to Google.* San Francisco, CA: Pfeiffer.

Alexander, L. (2009, October 26). Why college should take only three years. *Newsweek*, 26–29.

Allen, E. L. (1973, April 7). The 3 year baccalaureate. *The Journal of General Education* (Pennsylvania State University Press), 61–76.

Archibald, R. B., & Feldman, D. H. (2010). *Why does college cost so much?* New York, NY: Oxford University Press.

Arum, R., & Roksa, J. (2011). *Academically adrift: Limited learning on college campuses.* Chicago: University of Chicago Press.

Aud, S., Hussar, W., Kena, G., Bianco, K., Frohlich, L., Kemp, J., & Tahan, K. (2011). *The condition of education 2011* (NCES 2011-033). U.S. Department of Education, National Center for Education Statistics. Washington, DC: U.S. Government Printing Office.

Banta, T. W. (Ed.). (2007a). *Assessing student achievement in general education: Assessment Update collections.* San Francisco, CA: Jossey-Bass.

Banta, T. W. (Ed.). (2007b). *Assessing student learning in the disciplines: Assessment Update collections.* San Francisco, CA: Jossey-Bass.

Barr, R. B., & Tagg, J. (1995, November/December). From teaching to learning: A new paradigm for undergraduate education. *Change*, 13–25.

Basken, P., & Field, K. (2008, February 1). Sallie Mae tying loans to students' credit scores and colleges' graduation rates. *The Chronicle of Higher Education*, 54(21), A19.

Beckhard, R. (1969). *Organizational development: Strategies and models*. Reading, MA: Addison-Wesley.

Berger, J. B., & Lyon, S. C. (2005). Past and present: A historical look at retention. In A. Seidman (Ed.), *College student retention: Formula for student success*. Westport, CT: Praeger.

Bloom, B. S., Hastings, J. T., & Madaus, G. G. (1971). *Handbook on formative and summative evaluation of student learning*. New York, NY: McGraw-Hill.

Blumberg, P. (2008). *Developing learner-centered teachers: A practical guide for faculty*. San Francisco, CA: Jossey-Bass.

Bonk, C. (2009). *The world is open: How web technology is revolutionizing education*. San Francisco, CA: Jossey-Bass.

Boyatzis, R. E. (1982). *The competent manager: A model for effective performance*. New York, NY: Wiley.

Bradley, M., & Painchaud, S. (2009). Innovation in higher education at Southern New Hampshire University: The design, development, and success of a three year honors curriculum in business administration. In *Proceedings of the 14th Annual Conference* (pp. 29–47). Athens, Greece: European Council of Business Education.

Brubacher, J. S., & Rudy, W. (1976). *Higher education in transition* (3rd ed.). New York, NY: Harper & Row.

Cambridge, D. (2010). *Eportfolios for lifelong learning and assessment*. San Francisco, CA: Jossey-Bass.

Carnevale, A. P. (2008). A real analysis of real education. *Liberal Education* (Association of American Colleges and Universities), 94(4), 54–61.

Casner-Lotto, J., Rosenblum, E., & Wright, E. (2009). *The ill-prepared U.S. workforce*. Retrieved from https://www.shrm.org/Communities/Volunteer Resources/WebcastArchivesforVolunteerLeaders/Documents/Key_Findings _The_Ill-Prepared_US_Workforce.pdf

CEPH (Council on Education for Public Health). (2006). *Competencies and learning objectives*. Retrieved from http://www.ceph.org/pdf/Competencies_TA.pdf

Chronicle of Higher Education. (2010, November 5). Special issue: *Online Learning.* Retrieved from http://wiredcampus.chronicle.com/section/Online-Learning/491/

Cohen, A. M., & Kisker, C. B. (2010). *The shaping of American higher education: Emergence and growth of the contemporary system* (2nd ed.). San Francisco, CA: Jossey-Bass.

Collins, J. (2001). *Good to great.* New York, NY: Harper Collins.

Cooke, M., Irby, D. M., O'Brien, B. C., & Shulman, L. S. (2010). *Educating physicians: A call for reform of medical school and residency.* San Francisco, CA: Jossey-Bass.

Cooper, J. L., Robinson, P., & Ball, D. (Eds.). (2003). *Small group instruction in higher education: Lessons from the past, visions of the future.* Stillwater, OK: New Forums.

Council for Adult and Experiential Learning (CAEL). (2009). *Fueling the race to postsecondary success.* Retrieved from http://www.cael.org/pdf/PLA_Fueling-the-Race.pdf

Diamond, R. M. (2008). *Designing and assessing courses and curricula: A practical guide* (3rd ed.). San Francisco, CA: Jossey-Bass.

Dolence, M. G., & Norris, D. M. (1995). *Transforming higher education: A vision for learning in the 21st century.* Ann Arbor, MI: Society for College and University Planning.

DuFour, B., & DuFour, R. (2008). What is a PLC? Retrieved from http://thirteen celebration.org/blog/edblog/what-is-a-plc/17/DuFour

DuFour, R. (2004). What is a "professional learning community"? *Educational Leadership, 61*(8), 6–11.

DuFour, R., & Eaker, R. (1998). *Professional learning communities at work: Best practices for enhancing student achievement.* Bloomington, IN: Solution Tree.

ETS (Educational Testing Service). (2011). *Major field tests: Scores and reports.* Retrieved from http://www.ets.org/mft/scores

European Higher Education Area. (2011). About the Bologna Process. Retrieved from http://ehea.info

Evers, F. T., Rush, J. C., & Berdrow, I. (1998). *The bases of competence: Skills for lifelong learning and employability*. San Francisco: Jossey-Bass.

Fain, P. (2009, February 9). Gordon Gee says colleges face "reinvention or extinction." *The Chronicle of Higher Education*. Retrieved from http://chronicle .com/daily/2009/02/11131n.htm

Fischer, K. (2011, May 15). Crisis of confidence threatens colleges. *The Chronicle of Higher Education*. Retrieved from http://chronicle.com/article/Higher -Education-in-America-a/127530/?sid=at&utm_source=at&utm_medium=en

Gardiner, L. F. (1994). *Redesigning higher education: Producing dramatic gains in student learning*. ASHE-ERIC Higher Education Report No. 7. Washington, DC: Graduate School of Education and Human Development, George Washington University.

Gaston, P. (2010). *The challenge of Bologna*. Sterling, VA: Stylus.

Gordon, J. R. (2001). *Organizational behavior: A diagnostic approach*. Upper Saddle River, NJ: Prentice Hall.

Greenhow, C., Robelia, B., & Hughes, J. (2009). Web 2.0 and classroom research: What path should we take now? *Educational Researcher, 38*(4), 246–259. DOI: 10.3102/0013189X09336671

Hagedorn, L. S. (2005). How to define retention: A new look at an old problem. In A. Seidman (Ed.), *College student retention: Formula for student success*. Westport, CT: Praeger.

Johnson, D., & Johnson, F. (1975). *Joining together: Group theory and group skills*. Englewood Cliffs, NJ: Prentice-Hall.

Jones, E., Voorhees, R., & Paulson, K. (2002). *Defining and assessing learning: Exploring competency-based initiatives*. Washington, DC: Council of the National Postsecondary Education Cooperative. National Center for Education Statistics Publication: NCES 2002159. Retrieved from http://nces.ed.gov/ pubs2002/2002159.pdf

Katzenbach, J. R., & Smith, D. K. (1993). *The wisdom of teams*. New York, NY: Harper Business.

Keller, G. (2008). *Higher education and the new society*. Baltimore, MD: Johns Hopkins University Press.

Kiley, K. (2011, May 23). Discounting the bottom line. *Inside Higher Ed*. Retrieved from http://www.insidehighered.com/news/2011/05/23/nacubo _survey_finds_increased_tuition_discounting_led_to_financial_problems_during _the_recession

Knapp, L. G., Kelly-Reid, J. E., & Ginder, S. A. (2010). *Postsecondary institutions and price of attendance in the United States: Fall 2009, degrees and other awards conferred: 2008–09, and 12-month enrollment: 2008–09* (NCES 2010–161). U.S. Department of Education. Washington, DC: National Center for Education Statistics. Retrieved from http://nces.ed.gov/pubs2010/2010161.pdf

Kotter, J. (1996). *Leading change*. Boston, MA: Harvard Business School Press.

Kuh, G. D., Kinzie, J., Schuh, J. H., Whitt, E. J., and associates. (2010). *Student success in college: Creating the conditions that matter*. San Francisco, CA: Jossey-Bass.

Labonte, M. (2009, November 10). *U.S. economy in recession: Similarities to the differences from the past*. Congressional Research Service, R40198.

Lattuca, L., & Stark, J. (2009). *Shaping the college curriculum: Academic plans in context* (2nd ed.). San Francisco, CA: Jossey-Bass.

Lederman, D. (2009, February 10). Politicians praise and pressure colleges. *Inside Higher Ed*. Retrieved from http://www.insidehighered.com/news/2009/02/10/ace

Lincoln, Y. S., & Guba, E. G. (1985). *Naturalistic inquiry*. New York, NY: Sage.

Lumina Foundation for Education. (2011, January). *The degree qualifications profile*. Retrieved from http://www.luminafoundation.org/publications/The _Degree_Qualifications_Profile.pdf

NCES (National Center for Education Statistics). (2010a). Glossary. Retrieved from http://nces.ed.gov/ipeds/glossary/index.asp?id=77

NCES. (2010b). Table 36. First-time degree/certificate-seeking undergraduate retention rates at Title IV institutions, by attendance status and level and control of institution: United States, fall 2008. Retrieved from http://nces.ed.gov /das/library/tables_listings/showTable2005.asp?popup=true&tableID=6638&rt=p

NCES. (2010c). Table 33. Graduation rates at the 4-year or 2-year Title IV institution where the students started as full-time, first-time students, by race/ ethnicity, level of institution, gender, degree-granting status, and graduation rate component: United States, cohort years 2002 and 2005. Retrieved from http:// nces.ed.gov/das/library/tables_listings/showTable2005.asp?popup=true &tableID=6635&rt=p

NCHEMS (National Center for Higher Education Management Systems). (2010a). Retention rates: First-time college freshmen returning their second year. Retrieved from http://www.higheredinfo.org/dbrowser/?year=2008&level =nation&mode=data&state=0&submeasure=226

NCHEMS. (2010b). Graduation rates. Retrieved from http://www.higheredinfo .org/dbrowser/index.php?submeasure=27&year=2008&level=nation&mode =data&state=0

NEASC (New England Association of Schools and Colleges). (2001). *Report to the faculty, administration, trustees, students of Southern New Hampshire University.* Bedford, MA: NEASC.

NEASC. (2010a). *Statement on credits and degrees.* Retrieved from http://cihe.neasc.org/downloads/POLICIES/Pp90_Best_Practices_for_Elect. _Off._Degree_Cert._Prog.pdf

NEASC. (2010b). *Statement of best practices for electronically offered degree and certificate programs.* Retrieved from http://cihe.neasc.org/downloads/POLICIES /Pp110_StatementOnCredit.Degrees.pdf

Noble, D. F. (2002, March). Technology and the commodification of higher education. *Monthly Review,* 26–41.

Obama, B. (2011). *State of the Union address—2011.* Retrieved from http://www .whitehouse.gov/the-press-office/2011/01/25/remarks-president-state-union-address

Painchaud, M. (2010). *Academic consultancy/applied management experience* [Pamphlet]. Manchester, NH: Southern New Hampshire University. Document: OL 429 NPD 2010–2011.

Perry, M. (2010, November 5). Tomorrow's college: The classroom of the future features face to face, online and hybrid learning. And the future is here. *Chronicle of Higher Education*, Online Learning.

Prince, M. (2004). Does active learning work? A review of the research. *Journal of Engineering Education*, 93(3), 223–231.

Pritchard, M., Wilson, G., & Yamnitz, B. (2007). What predicts adjustment among college students? A longitudinal panel study. *Journal of American College Health*, 56. Retrieved from http://scholarworks.boisestate.edu/cgi /viewcontent.cgi?article=1005&context=psych_facpubs

Robinson, R. (2001, September). Calibrated peer review: An application to increase student reading and writing skills. *American Biology Teacher*, 63(7), 478–480.

Schein, E. H. (2010). *Organizational culture and leadership* (4th ed.). San Francisco, CA: Jossey-Bass.

Seidman, A. (Ed.) (2005). *College student retention: Formula for student success*. Westport, CT: ACE/Praeger.

Seidman, R. H., & Bradley, M. (2002). *A collaborative and competency-based three-year bachelor's degree: Empirical results*. American Educational Research Association Annual Meeting. ERIC Document Reproduction Service No. ED481060.

Shute, V. J. (2008). Focus on formative feedback. *Review of Educational Research*, 78(1), 153–189.

Smith, B. L., MacGregor, J., Matthews, R., & Gabelnick, F. (2004). *Learning communities: Reforming undergraduate education*. San Francisco, CA: Jossey-Bass.

Southern New Hampshire University (SNHU) School of Business. (2011). *Business competencies*. Retrieved from http://www.snhu.edu/361.asp

State of Rhode Island. (2009). *Three years to a college degree in Rhode Island* (Press Release). Retrieved from http://www.rilin.state.ri.us/News/pr1.asp?prid=5939

Student-Right-to-Know and Campus Security Act. (1990 November 8). Public Law 101–542. U.S. Code 1001.

Svinicki, W., & McKeachie, M. (2010). *McKeachie's teaching tips: Strategies, research, and theory for college and university teachers* (13th ed.). New York, NY: Cengage.

Tagg, J. (2003). *The learning paradigm college*. San Francisco, CA: Anker /Jossey-Bass.

Tinto, V. (1998). *Learning communities: Building gateways to student success*. Syracuse, NY: Syracuse University Press.

Tinto, V. (1999). Taking retention seriously: Rethinking the first year of college. *NACADA Journal, 19*(2), 5–9.

Tinto, V. (2006–2007). Research and practice of student retention: What next? *Journal of College Student Retention: Research, Theory and Practice, 8*(1), 1–19.

Twigg, C. A. (2003, September/October). Improving learning and reducing cost: New models for online learning. *EDUCAUSE Review, 38*(5), 30–38.

University of California. (2010). *University of California commission on the future: Final report*. Retrieved from http://ucfuture.universityofcalifornia.edu /presentations/cotf_final_report.pdf

Volkwein, J. F. (Ed.). (2010). *Assessing student outcomes: Why, who, what, how?* New Directions for Institutional Research, Assessment Supplement 2009. San Francisco, CA: Jossey-Bass.

Walvoord, B. E. (2010). *Assessment clear and simple: A practical guide for institutions, departments, and general education* (2nd ed.). San Francisco, CA: Jossey-Bass.

Weimer, M. (2002). *Learner-centered teaching: Five key changes to practice*. San Francisco, CA: Jossey-Bass.

Wellman, J. V., & Ehrlich, T. (Eds.) (2003a). *How the student credit hour shapes higher education: The tie that binds*. New Directions for Higher Education, No. 122. San Francisco, CA: Jossey-Bass.

Wellman, J. V., & Ehrlich, T. (2003b). Re-examining the sacrosanct credit hour. *Chronicle of Higher Education*, 50(5), B16.

Wildavsky, B. (2010). *The great brain race*. Princeton, NJ: Princeton University Press.

Wolf, P., & Hughes, J. (Eds). (2008). *Curriculum development in higher education: Faculty-driven processes and practices*. New Directions for Teaching and Learning, No. 112. San Francisco, CA: Jossey-Bass.

Zemke, R., Raines, C., & Filipczak, B. (2000). *Generations at work*. New York, NY: AMACOM/AMA Publications.

Zemsky, R., Wegner, G., & Massy, W. (2005). *Reworking the American university: Market-smart and mission-centered*. New Brunswick, NJ: Rutgers University Press.

Index

University of South Dakota, 11
U.S. Department of Education:
FIPSE grant from, for SNHU
three-year program, 67, 70;
recognition of three-year
bachelor's degrees by, 25

V
Value-added dimensions, 104–119;
academic themes, 106–107; active
teaching and learning, 110–113;
professional learning
communities, 107–110; student
assessment, 117–119; student
cohorts and learning communities,
104–105; student work groups,
106; virtual collaborative
environments, 113–117
Virtual collaborative environments,
104, 113–117, 121, 122–123,
148
Vision statements, 70–72
Volkwein, J. F., 90
Voorhees, R., 28, 30

W
Walvoord, B. E., 45, 87
"Web 2.0 and Classroom Research"
(Greenhow, Robelia, and
Hughes), 114

Wegner, G., xviii, 2, 139
Weimer, M., 111
Wellman, J. V., 26
"What Is a PLC?" (DuFour and
DuFour), 108
"What Is a 'Professional Learning
Community'" (DuFour), 108
Why Does College Cost So Much?
(Archibald and Feldman), xviii
Wildavsky, B., 22
Wilson, G., 75
The Wisdom of Teams (Katzenbach
and Smith), 54
Wolf, P., 32
Work groups, student, 103, 106
Workforce: data on SNHU
three-year-program graduates in,
98; entering, one year earlier, 86,
93; readiness to enter, 89–90, 147;
skills needed by, 66–67
The World Is Open (Bonk), 114
Wright, E., 98

Y
Yale, 7
Yamnitz, B., 75

Z
Zemke, R., 160
Zemsky, R., xviii, 2, 139